FEB 0 6 1992

J   Powers, Tom (Tom J.)
791   Special effects in the movies / by Tom Powers. --
.43   San Diego, CA : Lucent Books, c1989.
024   112 p. : ill. -- (Lucent overview series)
Pow

         Includes index.
         Bibliography: p. 103-105.
         04326059   LC:89012703 ISBN:1560061022 (lib. bdg.)

         1. Cinematography - Special effects. I. Title

213   92JAN06   33/ma   1-00951650

Special Effects in the Movies

Special Effects in the Movies

Look for these and other books in the Lucent
Overview series:

Special Effects in the Movies

by Tom Powers

LUCENT
B·O·O·K·S

LUCENT Overview Series

Library of Congress Cataloging-in-Publication Data

Powers, Tom (Tom J.)
  Special effects in the movies.

  (Lucent overview series)
  Bibliography: p.
  Includes index.
  Summary: Describes various techniques used by moviemakers
to create ''impossible'' situations and creatures that appear real to
the audience. Discusses mattes, glass painting, explosions, rear
screen projection, computer-enhancement, and make-up.
  1. Cinematography—Special effects—Juvenile literature.
[1. Cinematography—Special effects]
I. Title. II. Series.
TR858.P68 1989   791.43'024   89-12703
ISBN 1-56006-102-2

*For Patty who doesn't hear the words
but loves the special effects.*

Contents

CHAPTER ONE

"I Think We Got a Big Problem"

Steven Spielberg knew exactly what he wanted. The young movie director's 1984 film, *Indiana Jones and the Temple of Doom*, would open with a spectacular stunt involving an out-of-control airplane. The stunt would be difficult, and perhaps even dangerous, to film.

In the film's story, hero Indiana Jones has just escaped from the evil gangster Lao Che. Jones boards a small cargo plane, pausing in the hatchway to wave good-bye to Lao Che. Lao Che responds with a wicked smile and a signal to the pilots. Jones does not realize that Lao Che's men are flying the airplane.

At the very start of the film, Jones befriended an orphan boy named Short Round and a beautiful singer named Willie. Now the three friends doze off as their plane soars over the Great Wall of China. Lao Che's pilots wait for the right moment. They release a valve that dumps the plane's fuel supply, then parachute out of the airplane.

Willie wakes up first and realizes that no one is flying the airplane. She rouses Indy and Short Round, but there is nothing they can do. The plane is going to crash. As Willie points in silent horror, one of the plane's wheels skims a snowy mountaintop. An even higher mountain looms straight ahead. "I think we got a big problem," says Indiana Jones.

At the last moment, the three friends bail out of the plane in a large rubber life raft. They land safely in the snow just as their plane explodes against a mountain. Then a whole new set of adventures begins.

Spielberg knew that this scene would require the art of special effects—the art of making impossible, dangerous scenes look real. To show his special effects crew how he wanted the scene to look, Spielberg made a storyboard, a series of drawings that showed every change in the scene's action. When Spielberg finished drawing his rough sketches, he turned them over to an artist who filled in the details. The finished storyboard looked like a series of drawings from a comic book.

The magic of Dennis Muren

Making movies is a complex business, and a director like Steven Spielberg has to communicate with actors, cinematographers (camera operators), technical experts, and business people. Drawing storyboards helps Spielberg explain his ideas to people. "In the planning stage," Spielberg says, "I'm a storyteller, a cinematographer, and an editor. *Then* I have to work with people and get it all across to them. You see, I have no idea how to engineer the things I have in my head."

One of the first people to whom Spielberg showed the film's storyboard was Dennis Muren, the man in charge of *Indiana Jones*'s special effects. Muren is a special effects technician who has been making films since he was ten years old. Spielberg and Muren had worked together before, on *E.T.*, the biggest money-making film ever made. Each man knew what to expect from the other. "If Dennis came up with something that was different from the approved storyboards," said a co-worker, "he was not afraid to try it—even without Steven's prior approval. Generally it looked great and Steven was totally happy with it."

Muren worked for Industrial Light and Magic, a company based in northern California's Marin County. The company had been organized by George Lucas to design special effects for the 1977 film *Star Wars*. That film helped Lucas become one of the most successful moviemakers of all time. Now Lucas was acting as co-producer and co-writer of *Indiana Jones and the Temple of Doom*.

Industrial Light and Magic—or ILM—was once known as "the Country Club" because everyone came to work in T-shirts, shorts, and floppy beach thongs. ILM soon built a reputation as the best special effects company in the film industry. One of the first people hired by ILM was Dennis Muren.

Muren knew that it was easy to draw pictures of an exciting scene like the airplane crash in *Indiana Jones*. To bring those pictures to life would be a much more difficult problem. The airplane crash in *Indiana Jones* was just one of hundreds of special effects in the film. Each effect, no matter how spectacular, still had to look real. Dennis Muren knew that Steven Spielberg and George Lucas would not settle for less. After spending hours or even days getting a scene to look just right, Muren would often tell his crew, "That looks good. Now let's make it look natural."

Muren showed Spielberg's drawings of the airplane crash to his ILM crew of special effects artists. He asked them first to consider

Moviemaker Steven Spielberg has directed many well-known movies that use fantastic special effects. These movies include E.T., Jaws, *and* Indiana Jones and the Last Crusade.

the dramatic value of the scene. Was the scene really effective? Would it look good on film? Would it fit together with the rest of the story?

Then Muren asked his crew to evaluate the cost of shooting the scene. (To ''shoot'' a scene means to photograph it. A film ''shot'' is the picture that the camera photographs.) Spielberg sometimes dreamed up scenes that were just too expensive to shoot. In this scene, for instance, he wanted to blow up an old and valuable airplane. Was that necessary?

Combining special effects techniques

Finally, the special effects crew had to decide whether to use physical effects such as actually blowing up the plane, optical effects (different kinds of trick photography), or miniatures and models.

If ILM decided to use miniatures, Muren faced a whole new set of problems. The special effects crew would have to build a tiny plane and mountains to match it. Then the camera crew would have to film the miniatures from just the right angles and with just the right lighting. For the special effects to be successful, full-scale, miniature, and optical effects all had to look the same. They had to look *real*.

In the end, Muren and his ILM crew decided to use a combination of techniques. They would use miniatures, optical effects, and full-scale physical effects. Muren suggested building a three-foot long model of Lao Che's old Ford trimotor cargo plane. A real Ford trimotor would be used for some shots, as when Indiana Jones waves good-bye at the airport. The model, however, would be used for crashing into the mountain.

Since the ILM crew was also busy shooting effects for the film *Star Trek III: The Search for Spock* they did not have time to do all the special effects needed for *Indiana Jones*. So another special effects company was hired to build a model of the Great Wall of China. (Taking the full-sized plane to China would have cost ILM too much money. Part of the reason filmmakers use special effects is to save money on difficult shots.)

Lights were placed low and behind this model, so the sun appeared to be coming up over the Great Wall. The model airplane was hung from wires and made to move in a jerky fashion over the model of the Great Wall. That made it look like the airplane was being rocked by the wind.

A separate full-sized model was built for the cockpit of the airplane. This cockpit was placed on giant inner tubes, which could be pumped up and down to duplicate the plane's movement. Shots looking out

Model airplanes hang from wires over miniature mountains. These airplanes will appear real to movie viewers once the wires and wooden grid are hidden from view.

from the cockpit window—for instance, when Indiana Jones sees the plane's propellers stop—were taken from the real plane flying over the Sierra Nevada mountain range in California.

The shot of the airplane's wheel striking the mountaintop was too risky to attempt with a real airplane and live actors. So the special effects crew built a small mountaintop out of two-foot chunks of coal. They covered this coal peak with baking soda (to look like snow), and again they controlled the model plane with wires. Muren coated the wires with a felt-tipped marker to make them harder to see. When

The perfected model airplane scene. The wires holding up the "flying" planes and the wooden grid are no longer visible. The miniature scene, built to scale, gives the illusion of life-size objects seen from a distance.

the model plane's wheel hit the mountaintop, the wheel spun and snow went flying. On-screen, the shot lasts only one second, but it makes audiences gasp.

The final problem in this scene came with the plane crash. The crew realized that their airplane model was too big to be shown against a small model mountain range. To make the mountains match the plane, the crew would have to build a model mountain range that would cover the entire ILM parking lot. They did not want to do this, so they decided to build a second model plane, half as big as the first.

An explosive afterthought

Muren was afraid that when the model plane crashed, parts of it would be left dangling from the wires that held it up. The audience would see these bits of plane dangling in the air, and that would ruin the illusion of a real crash. He therefore decided to build a five-foot-long mechanical arm that *pulled* the model into the mountain. The camera operator shot the plane from behind, so that viewers could not see the mechanical arm.

Since the plane, according to the story, was out of fuel, the special effects crew did not think it should explode. Later, when all the shots were filmed and the scene was put together, Spielberg and Lucas decided an explosion *was* needed. Since the model mountain had been torn down, an explosion was added to the film by a special process called optical printing. Optical printing allows filmmakers to rephotograph film that has already been shot—to take a picture of a picture. Through optical printing, filmmakers can add extra effects or make changes in the size and shape of the image, or picture, that appears on the film.

ILM had lots of explosions in its film library. The special effects crew simply laid a shot of an explosion over the shot of the plane crash. Then they optically printed the two shots together. The final shot came out looking just like a real plane exploding.

Two different special effects companies and dozens of people worked on this one scene from *Indiana Jones and the Temple of Doom*. On-screen, the scene runs about four and a half minutes from takeoff to plane crash. All the special effects shots taken together run for only one minute.

If one looks at the film carefully, for instance by stopping and starting it on a videotape machine, it is almost impossible to tell which shots are real and which are special effects. On a big screen, with the film whizzing by, audiences have no time to think about how the film was made. They simply are caught up in the adventures of Indiana Jones. That, of course, is exactly what Dennis Muren, George Lucas, and Steven Spielberg wanted.

CHAPTER TWO

Dreams and Screams

Movies have always had the power to make people believe that what they are seeing on-screen is really happening. Special effects add to that power. By using special effects, filmmakers make "impossible" scenes look real.

Through special effects, filmmakers have shown actors parting the waters of the Red Sea, flying to distant planets, and chopping off heads on Friday the 13th. Special effects have also allowed filmmakers to create strange, unreal images—people disappearing, cloud cities, giant apes, and telephones with teeth. Such images have been used to thrill, shock, and entertain audiences. They have also been used to show viewers some of their most deeply hidden dreams and fears, such as fear of death, aging, illness, loneliness, being different, and being out of control of a situation.

The very first films did not need to use special effects to make audiences believe that what they were seeing was real. When members of the first film audience in 1895 saw a moving picture of a train heading toward them, they dove for cover—even though the train in that early silent film was not making any noise. Audiences quickly learned, however, that movies could not hurt them. So filmmakers just as quickly came up with new ways to keep audiences thrilled, scared, and ducking for cover.

Nearly fifty years after *The Arrival of a Train* was first shown, the makers of a jungle film called *Bwana Devil* (1952) used a special effect called three-dimensional photography (3-D) to send viewers diving under their seats. The 3-D process makes the image on the screen pop right out at the audience. Modern Hollywood producers are still using 3-D to thrill viewers. In the 1983 film *Jaws 3-D*, a giant shark seems to lunge right out of the screen. For the modern viewers watching *Jaws 3-D*, the movie's power to fool people is as strong as it was for the first film audience.

Early uses of special effects

The first movies were made around 1895 by the Lumiere brothers in France and by American inventors Thomas Edison and W.K.L. Dickson, who built a small film studio in East Orange, New Jersey. These pioneers, and the cameramen who worked for them, quickly learned that camera tricks could add to the fun and excitement of the movies. Film historians think that some camera tricks like fast, slow, and reverse motion may have been discovered by accident when the camera got stuck or was run incorrectly. The resulting shots were the first "special effects."

Early special effects often were funny or educational. Shots of people disappearing or walking backward made audiences laugh. Shots of animals moving in slow motion or buildings being constructed in fast motion gave audiences a new understanding of the world around them. For the first time, people could see nature slowed down and human accomplishments sped up.

The first special effect shown to an audience probably was an 1896 film of a wall crumbling into rubble, then suddenly building itself back up again. To achieve this special effect, the filmmaker photographed a wall being demolished. Then he ran the film backward to show the wall being "rebuilt." *Demolition of a Wall* was a simple trick, but no one in the audience at that time had ever seen anything like it.

Early filmmakers often *wanted* audiences to notice the various special effects that they used. The whole point of *Demolition of a*

Wall was to let viewers see the wall rebuilding itself. Before long, however, filmmakers began to feel that special effects worked best when they were invisible, that is, when the audience could not tell that a special effect had been used. Invisible special effects allowed audiences to pay attention to a film's story without thinking about how the film was made.

Some early filmmakers used invisible special effects to frighten and shock people. They knew that people would pay to be shocked as long as they were not in any real danger. An 1895 film called *The Execution of Mary Queen of Scots* startled audiences by showing them something they did not expect to see. In this short film, Queen Mary was forced to kneel and place her head on a chopping block. A hooded executioner raised his axe, swung—and chopped the queen's head off. Audiences screamed in horror at the sight.

Of course, the filmmakers had played a trick on the audience. While they were shooting the film, the filmmakers stopped the camera for a moment. They substituted a dummy for the actress playing Queen Mary. Then they started filming again. When the film was shown

The Lumiere Brothers were Europe's first moviemakers. These film pioneers quickly discovered the excitement special effects added to their work.

COURTESY OF LUCASFILM LTD.

A special effects technician prepares the model actors and mine car used to film the heart-stopping chase in Indiana Jones and the Temple of Doom.

on-screen, the switch from actress to dummy happened in an instant. No one in the audience could tell that the switch had been made.

Nearly ninety years later, Steven Spielberg used the same technique in the famous mine-car chase in *Indiana Jones and the Temple of Doom*. In close shots of the speeding mine cars, Spielberg used live actors. In more distant—and more dangerous—shots, he substituted model figures for the actors playing Indy, Short Round, and Willie. By substituting models for the actors, Spielberg was able to show viewers a faster, scarier, more dangerous ride than he could have filmed if he had used live actors. The switches from actors to models take place many times throughout the scene, yet they are very hard to detect.

Filmmakers often refer to special effects as ''gags'' because special effects are used to fool audiences. A good gag makes an audience think it is seeing something that is really happening rather than a cleverly disguised special effect. Carefully planned gags, like the mine-car chase in *Indiana Jones* or the head chopping in *Mary Queen of Scots*, help filmmakers convince audiences that they are watching shockingly real scenes that most viewers would never see anyplace else.

Besides helping filmmakers make scenes look real, special effects allow filmmakers to show audiences how their dreams and fantasies might look. In real life, no one gets to fly like Superman or disappear like the Invisible Man. No one knows what it is like to pilot a starfighter or to meet creatures from other planets (although some people say they have!). But special effects in movies like *Superman*, *The Invisible Kid*, *Star Trek*, and *The Last Starfighter* can make dreams like these become real.

Exposing our fears on film

At other times, filmmakers use special effects to tap into people's hidden fears. Most people are afraid of death and sickness, and no one likes to feel trapped or embarrassed. These are powerful feelings, so powerful that people are sometimes uncomfortable thinking or talking about them. Filmmakers know that audiences will pay to see how movie characters deal with their worst fears and strongest feelings. That fear might be the loneliness experienced by a deformed boy in *Mask* or the terror of a man who sees his skin falling off as he turns into a giant fly in *The fly*. Both these films, one a true story and the other a science fiction fantasy, show characters who have to deal with the emotional and physical pain of disease.

Filmmakers often use special effects to exaggerate an audience's dreams or fears—to make them larger or scarier than real life. In real life, no one worries about having to jump out of an airplane in a rubber life raft the way Indiana Jones does. Unlike Indiana Jones, most movie viewers have never been lowered into pits of boiling oil or crushed by giant rocks. They do not know what it is like to be trapped in dark corridors crawling with beetles and scorpions, or to be served chilled monkey brains for dessert.

Almost everyone, however, knows what it is like to be afraid of heights or to dream about falling through the air. Most people know what it is like to be burned or to feel suffocated, to be unable to catch one's breath. Everyone has been annoyed by insects or has eaten foul-tasting food. When viewers watch Indiana Jones survive torments and dangers far worse than anything they have ever imagined, their own fears seem a little less frightening by comparison.

The art of special effects also helps filmmakers show everyday problems in ways that are bigger than life. The title character in the film

Actor David Naughton's character expresses horror as he changes into a werewolf in an American Werewolf in London. *People don't turn into animals in real life.*

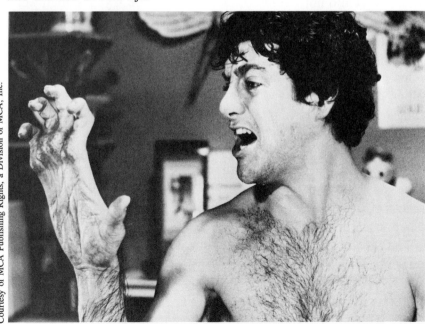

Carrie, for instance, does not simply get laughed at by her fellow high school students; she gets drenched in pig's blood in the middle of the prom. In response, Carrie burns down the school gymnasium. The hero of *The fly* does not just get sick; his body falls apart as he turns into a frightening monster. In *Teen Wolf* and *An American Werewolf in London*, the heroes do not simply feel different from their friends; they turn into hairy beasts who try to kill the people they love. All these films show "bigger than life" problems, yet they really are dealing with very basic human fears: fears of embarrassment, illness, loneliness, and death.

Violence and visitors

Sometimes everyone in a society shares the same worry or fear. When the United States was fighting the war in Vietnam, for instance, Americans knew that young men were dying in horrible ways—but most people did not want to think about how these young men were suffering. As a result, very few Vietnam War films were made until a long time after the war was over. War movies like *Platoon* did not appear until ten years later.

Instead, filmmakers made other kinds of films—westerns, horror films, gangster films, and science fiction movies—but they began to make these movies very bloody. Movies during the 1960s and 1970s invited viewers to look at the *violence* of war without having to look at pictures of war itself. Starting with *Bonnie and Clyde* in 1967 and *The Wild Bunch* in 1968, people in movies no longer simply got shot; they got ripped apart by exploding bullets. New developments in special effects made it possible to show the physical damage that takes place when someone is shot.

This violent trend in movies continued long after the Vietnam War was over. In *Scanners* (1981), a man's head exploded. In *Alien* (1979) and *The Thing* (1982), monsters erupted from inside people's bodies. All these movies seemed to be asking audiences to look at the horror of violence and bloodshed—the horror that people tried not to think about during the Vietnam War and for a long time afterward.

More recently, Americans have faced a different situation: the new wave of immigrants coming to this country. People from foreign countries bring new languages and customs to the United States. They often work long hours at low-paying jobs in order to get ahead in their new country. Some Americans feel uncomfortable with these immigrants because the new arrivals seem different and strange. Other Americans fear that the new immigrants will take their jobs away or change the American way of life.

No one wants to express this feeling, however. Many Americans know that their parents or grandparents were once new arrivals, too. Still, the feeling of being uncomfortable with strangers has bothered Americans in the 1980s, and it has begun to be expressed in movies— but not directly.

Instead of dealing with viewers' worries about strangers from other countries, many movies in the 1980s have told stories about people from other worlds. Science fiction films like *E.T.*, **batteries not included*, *Gremlins*, *Close Encounters of the Third Kind*, *V*, and *The Brother from Another Planet* all deal with the ways Americans might respond to visitors from distant worlds. Horror film director George Romero has said that his scary "living dead" films (*Night of the Living Dead*, *Dawn of the Dead*, and *Day of the Dead*) are really stories about what happens when a new group of people takes over a society.

Strangely human characters

All these films use special effects to make sure that their "foreign" characters look different from ordinary human beings. Their odd looks, however, do not stop the characters from acting human. The gremlins like to party, and E.T. loves candy. The "living dead" haunt a shopping mall because they seem to remember hanging out in malls when they were alive. As one character says to another, the mall used to be "an important place" in their lives. Special effects in these movies allow viewers to examine their confused feelings toward strangers who might look different but still have human faults and virtues.

For more than ninety years, special effects in movies have helped filmmakers create people, places, and events that are so wonderful, frightening, or impossible that they could exist only in dreams and nightmares—or on a movie screen. Today's audiences may dream about flying starships rather than magic carpets. They may be frightened more by violence in their neighborhoods than by giant apes or prehistoric dinosaurs. But like audiences in the past, audiences today still turn to the movies to see their fears and dreams made real through the magic of special effects.

CHAPTER THREE

How to Make Bicycles Fly

The matte shot, or mask as it sometimes is called, is one of the oldest special effects. A matte blocks out (or "masks") part of the image, the picture that the camera films. The part of the image that is blocked out by a matte looks like a black hole. This hole can be filled in later with details, actions, or characters that have been filmed separately.

The matte shot is the special effect that makes it possible to show a real Indiana Jones hanging from the face of a fake cliff, or to place real people inside tiny models in *2001*. Mattes allow Princess Leia to race her speeder bike through the redwoods in *Return of the Jedi*, and E.T. and Elliot to fly across the sky on Elliot's bicycle. Matte shots allow filmmakers to create fantastic scenes that otherwise would be too expensive, or even impossible, to film.

Simple mattes

In its simplest form, a matte is a black card held in front of the camera lens. This matte card can have many different shapes. It can be used to cover a large part of the image or just a small part, like a window or doorway. When a camera operator photographs a scene, the area hidden behind the matte card does not show up on the filmed image.

Here is an example of a simple matte. Suppose a character in a movie looks through a keyhole. To show the audience the character's point of view (what the character sees), the filmmaker first takes a black matte card and cuts an opening in the shape of a keyhole. Then she or he places this matte card in front of the camera lens. The camera shoots through the hole in the matte card, and the resulting image looks like a scene filmed through a keyhole.

One of the earliest uses of mattes occurred in the 1903 film *The Great Train Robbery*. The director of this film used a matte to combine separate shots of a telegraph office and of a train arriving outside. To do this, the director "matted out" the office window—he placed a matte card in front of the camera lens, covering just that part of the image where the window would appear. Later, the director added a shot of a train to the part of the image that had been blocked out. When the shot of the office and the shot of the train were combined, it looked like the train was arriving right outside the office window. This special effect made audiences think they were watching a scene filmed from inside a real telegraph office. In fact, the scene had been filmed on a set in Thomas Edison's New Jersey studio.

Split-screen mattes

Sixty-five years after *The Great Train Robbery*, director Stanley Kubrick used this same special effect in his epic *2001: A Space Odyssey*. First, Kubrick filmed the outside of a tiny space station, using mattes to block out the space station's windows. Later, shots of people were added to these blocked-out spaces. When the shots of the people were combined with the shots of the space station, it looked like people were walking around inside the space station.

A split-screen matte is a type of matte often used to make characters appear on-screen with themselves. This technique was used in the 1945 film *Wonder Man*, so that the actor Danny Kaye could play twin brothers. For scenes where the twins appeared together, a split-screen matte was used. In these scenes, the matte card split the screen

Courtesy of Turner Entertainment

The space station in 2001: A Space Odyssey *is an example of how filmmakers use mattes to put real people inside model spaceships. Through the ship's windows, the audience sees the pilots and passengers moving about inside.*

right down the middle, blocking out one side.

In these split-screen scenes, Danny Kaye first was filmed on the right side of the scene, with a matte placed over the left side of the camera lens. This matte permitted only the right side of the scene to be recorded.

After the scene was shot, the cameraman shifted the matte card to block out the right side of the scene, the part of the action that had just been filmed. He then rewound the film in the camera to the starting point and double-exposed it—he shot the film a second time.

In this second run-through, Danny Kaye entered from the left side of the scene and stayed on the left side. Kaye had to time his words and gestures to fit the pauses and actions of his "twin brother," the character he played on the right side of the screen in the first run-through. Later, when the film was projected, and both halves of the action were seen together, it appeared that Kaye was talking to his

Danny Kaye peers at his "twin brother" in the 1945 film Wonder Man. *Split-screen mattes create the illusion that one actor is in two or more places in one scene.*

twin brother. The split-screen matte made this possible.

The silent film comedian Buster Keaton once used mattes for a similar split-screen effect, but he split the screen in many more places. In his 1921 film *The Playhouse*, Keaton played nine different characters, all of them on-screen at the same time. In *Gone with the Wind* (1939), a whole crowd was doubled in size by using a split-screen matte. The same people were filmed first on one side of the screen, then on the other.

Traveling mattes

The filming of *Wonder Man* required other, more complicated types of mattes. In the final film, the twins played by Danny Kaye did not always stay on separate sides of the screen. Special effects engineer John Fulton (whose father created special effects for *Gone with the Wind*) won an Academy Award for developing traveling mattes that allowed Kaye to move about freely.

Like other mattes, a traveling matte blocks out part of the film image, but it blocks out a moving part. For example, suppose a director wants to block out the part of an image occupied by a person who is walking around. To block out this part of the image—and to keep blocking it out as the person walks around—the director needs to use a matte that moves just as the person moves. A black card held in front of the lens would not work very well. So a traveling matte must be made from something other than a black card, something that moves. The trick, as John Fulton discovered, was to make traveling mattes from moving pictures.

Fulton made his traveling mattes from moving images of Danny Kaye. He turned these images into silhouettes, solid black figures in the shape of the actor. These silhouettes were used to block out spaces in scenes that had been filmed. Real moving images of Danny Kaye were then inserted into these spaces.

This traveling matte process, which involves many separate steps, has now become a common technique in films that use special effects.

Mary Poppins flying with her umbrella and Elliot and E.T. bicycling across the sky are examples of shots filmed using traveling mattes. So are television's Tidy-Bowl man rowing across the toilet tank and Princess Leia riding her speeder bike through the redwoods in *Return of the Jedi*. The scene with tiny Beetlejuice talking to his life-sized neighbors, when they discover the obnoxious little ghost living in a tabletop model of their village, was also done with traveling mattes.

The blue-screen method

Many traveling mattes are made by the blue-screen method. This method involves filming characters—such as the brownies in *Willow*—in front of a bright blue screen. The blue-screen method works because certain types of motion picture film do not show the color blue. That means that only the characters in a blue-screen shot are photographed by the camera. From these shots it is easy to make the silhouettes of characters needed for traveling mattes. Later, the mattes can be used to add the characters to scenes in a film, following the same process used in the making of *Wonder Man*.

A good example of a traveling matte made by the blue-screen method occurred early in *Return of the Jedi*. In that film, Princess Leia escaped from Imperial stormtroopers on a stolen speeder bike that moved a few feet above the ground. Such a speeder bike was impossible to build, so the scene was turned over to the Industrial Light and Magic special effects crew.

Carrie Fisher, playing Princess Leia, was filmed sitting on a model speeder bike in front of a bright blue screen. A large fan was used to blow back Fisher's hair, adding to the impression that she was actually moving. For this shot, the camera operator used a type of color film that would not photograph the color blue, the color in the background screen. Therefore only Princess Leia and the bike were photographed by the camera.

This left the filmmakers with an image they could use in two ways. First, the shot of Princess Leia (in a black silhouette) was used as

Using traveling mattes to create special effects involves several steps. Here, Princess Leia (actress Carrie Fisher) and a passenger from Return of the Jedi *are filmed in front of a blue screen to obtain a silhouette. This silhouette then becomes a matte that will be added to the forest background scene.*

a traveling matte to block out a section of other shots, which were filmed on location in the California redwoods. Then the same image of Princess Leia was inserted into the space created by the traveling matte.

ILM called on Dennis Muren to supervise the filming of the redwoods sequence. Muren told his camera operator to walk slowly through the redwoods, filming at the rate of one picture every few seconds.

Motion picture cameras work just like snapshot cameras, except that they take lots of pictures in a very short time. Motion picture cameras normally shoot twenty-four pictures—or frames—every second. A camera operator walking through the redwoods, filming at the normal speed, might walk just a foot or two while he took those twenty-four pictures. If he slowed down the camera speed, however, he might be able to walk fifty feet while he filmed the same

In the final scene from Return of the Jedi *Princess Leia and her passenger have been placed among the redwoods.*

number of pictures. This is what Dennis Muren's camera operator did. When the film that was photographed at a slower-than-normal speed was shown on-screen, the action looked sped up. Fifty feet of redwoods sped past the viewer in one second, rather than just one or two feet of the forest, as would have been the case if the shot had been filmed at normal speed.

Muren's sped-up shots of the redwoods gave viewers the feeling that giant trees were zipping past at 120 miles an hour. When shots of the speeder bike were matted into the redwood shots, Princess Leia seemed to be hurtling through the woods at dangerous speeds.

Matte lines outline a problem

In developing traveling mattes, filmmakers must go through several steps. Television directors, on the other hand, can create similar effects instantly. For instance, when a television weather forecaster points at a weather map behind him or her, the map often is not really there. That is why he or she sometimes seems unsure just where to point. The weather forecaster actually is standing in front of a blue screen, while the map is being filmed in a different part of the studio. The images of the map and the forecaster are combined electronically in the television camera, creating the picture that viewers see at home.

The blue-screen method of making mattes sometimes causes viewers to notice that special effects are being used. Any matte can leave a matte line on the final image. A matte line is a line that makes a figure stand out from the background or causes viewers to notice where two shots have been joined together. Blue-screen matte lines are particularly noticeable. On television, when "Star Trek's" Captain Kirk is "beamed up" or the weather forecaster stands in front of a map that isn't there, their bodies often have thin, glowing lines around them. These are the blue-screen matte lines. The same thing happens in movies. One problem many viewers found with *Willow* was that the matte lines around the brownies Rool and Franjean were particularly noticeable.

Courtesy of Boss Film Corporation

Tom Noonan as Frankenstein in Monster Squad *is not so scary when we see him hanging by wires before an empty blue screen. This step in the traveling matte process makes possible a thrilling effect on the movie screen.*

Whenever they can, directors try to use character movement or natural breaks in the scene (a road or a window frame, for instance) to hide the lines that show up between separately filmed shots that have been joined together through the use of mattes. In the last scene of *Raiders of the Lost Ark*, for instance, a matte was used to combine a shot of a workman pushing a cart with a shot of a huge warehouse. The workman seems to be moving down the middle aisle of the warehouse, pushing his load past other huge wooden boxes.

The man's movement helps distract audiences from noticing the lines that run between the shot of the warehouse and the shot of the workman.

This last shot of *Raiders of the Lost Ark* also contains another special effect. The entire warehouse did not exist. Only the shot of the workman coming down the aisle was real. The rest of the image was a painting!

CHAPTER FOUR

Castles in the Air

A photographer named Norman Dawn may have been the first person to use matte paintings in movies. When Dawn went to make his 1907 film *California Missions*, he found that many of the old California churches were in bad shape. Dawn wanted the missions to look like new, so he came up with a clever trick.

If a mission tower had fallen down or a roof had collapsed, Dawn painted the tower or the roof on a piece of glass. This painting was a kind of matte. It blocked out part of the image, while the part that was to be filmed could be seen clearly through the glass. Dawn placed the matte painting in front of his movie camera, being careful to position the painted tower or roof in line with the actual church. Then he filmed through the glass, recording the real church and its painted additions at the same time. In the finished film the old missions looked like new.

Dawn went on to work for a number of Hollywood film studios. He designed 861 special effects shots durings his sixty-three-year career. He also trained many young studio artists to carry on his techniques. Dawn helped make matte paintings one of the most important special effects techniques in movies.

The technique of modern matte painting

Today, special effects studios like Industrial Light and Magic rely heavily on matte paintings. ILM matte artists create fantastic landscapes, like the cliffside in *Indiana Jones and the Temple of Doom*, the Cloud City in *The Empire Strikes Back*, and Bavmorda's castle in *Willow*. When E.T. looked out over the city at night, what he saw was in fact a giant painting. (As a joke, matte artist Chris Evans included a street with "every fast-food chain in America on it.") In each of these landscapes the artist left an empty space in the matte painting where live-action shots could be inserted later.

Matte paintings are done on canvas, fiberboard, or glass. ILM's matte painters prefer to work on glass. Its flat surface is easy to paint on and easy to scrape off when new elements have to be optically added to the painting.

A perfect match goes unnoticed

It takes about two weeks for an ILM artist to produce a matte painting. A normal-sized ILM matte painting is two and a half feet by six feet—big enough for the artist to include plenty of believable details. A matte painter must be able to create a painting that looks as real as a photograph from a distance. Up close, however, matte paintings have a less polished appearance. This is because a painting that looks too real will not match the slightly grainy image recorded by motion picture film.

Matching a matte painting with a scene filmed on a studio set (the area where actors perform) is one of the matte artist's most difficult jobs. Matte artists have to consider the light, color, size, and shape of the moving images for which they are providing backgrounds. For this reason, many matte artists prefer to use oil paints rather than acrylic paints. Acrylic paints are easy to use and they dry quickly, but they sometimes dry to a slightly different color. That means that an artist using acrylic paints does not know whether his work will match the colors of the filmed image. If a painting is to be combined with a live-action shot, colors and lines must match perfectly.

The warehouse shot at the end of *Raiders of the Lost Ark* is a good example of a matte painting that fits perfectly with a scene's live action. This shot stays on the screen for thirty seconds. Most matte paintings cannot be held on-screen for longer than ten seconds without viewers realizing that they are looking at a painting. Matte artist Michael Pangrazio is proud that few viewers recognized his contribution to this final shot of *Raiders*.

Not all matte paintings are successful. One of Pangrazio's least favorite matte paintings is the ''Eden Cave'' scene that he painted for *Star Trek II: The Wrath of Khan*. In this scene, Captain Kirk is taken to a beautiful, gardenlike cave. The cave is supposed to show Kirk how a new scientific discovery called Project Genesis can turn a barren planet into a lush green world.

Matte artist Matthew Yurichich paints a matte for the movie Solarbabies. *A matte artist considers his work a success when the audience doesn't notice that the scene is a painting.*

The landscapes for the Eden Cave scene were painted by Michael Pangrazio and his fellow matte artist Chris Evans. The artists complained that they were never told how their paintings would blend in with the live-action shots of Captain Kirk. They did not understand the function their paintings were supposed to serve. Also, the matted areas of the paintings—the areas that the artists left blank for live-action shots—were very small. Because these areas were so small, there was little room for movement in the shots. As a result, there was not much to distract the viewers' attention from the painted parts of the scene.

A hidden art

Good matte painters like Michael Pangrazio and Chris Evans are always more concerned with the final product—the moving picture image that is shown to audiences—than they are with their own paintings. Matte painters often create beautiful works of art, but they are ready to scrape holes in their paintings, change them, or cover them to start new works if that is what a director wants.

Pangrazio once presented several of his paintings to a director who had a reputation for being difficult to please. The director secretly admired Pangrazio's work, but he still wanted to show the artist who was in charge, so he suggested some minor changes. Pangrazio picked up a ballpoint pen and began sketching the director's changes right on the surface of his paintings. The director was shocked by Pangrazio's willingness to alter his beautiful artwork.

Producer George Lucas, the founder of Industrial Light and Magic, loves to use matte paintings in his films. He thinks that some of his artists' works should be saved so that people can study and appreciate them in the future. Lucas has assigned one ILM worker the job of finding especially beautiful matte paintings and locking them away before the matte artists can change them, scrape them clean, or paint over them.

Chris Evans warns new matte painters that most of their work will

C3PO and R2D2 from Star Wars *have a long walk ahead of them. Or do they? The scene in the distance is a matte painting. This painting must match the foreground scene perfectly.*

remain "hidden." It will not be appreciated by viewers in the way that paintings normally are appreciated. Like most other special effects craftspeople, matte painters hope that audiences will not notice their work. The movie classic *Gone with the Wind* has been enjoyed by millions of viewers. Few people, however, are aware that more than one hundred shots in that film make use of matte paintings.

George Lucas used only thirteen matte paintings in seventeen shots in *Star Wars*—but they were shots that give the film a romantic, fairy-tale quality. When Luke Skywalker and Princess Leia swing across a bottomless shaft in the Death Star, they are really only a few feet above the ground. The "bottomless shaft" was a painting that was added to the matted-out lower part of the image.

Nothing's impossible

A 1941 film called *Citizen Kane* used a huge number of mattes, matte paintings, and other special effects to make sets seem much larger than they really were. The film was directed by Orson Welles, who was twenty-five years old at the time. Welles was new to film-making, and he did not understand that some things "could not be done." With the help of a special effects wizard named Linwood Dunn and a cameraman named Gregg Toland, Welles made a film that was full of "impossible" shots. Many of these shots involved the use of mattes and matte paintings to create huge rooms, a castle, and even a gigantic warehouse, which was the inspiration for the closing shot of *Raiders of the Lost Ark*.

Today many critics call *Citizen Kane* the greatest film of all time. Looking back at *Citizen Kane*, Dunn remembered what he told Welles about the art of special effects. "Nothing's impossible," Dunn said to Welles. "It's a matter of time and money and how good is it going to look?"

CHAPTER FIVE

Tiny Monsters

Like matte paintings, models and miniatures allow filmmakers to design shots that otherwise would be impossible to film. For example, the Rancor Pit monster that battled Luke Skywalker in *Return of the Jedi* was really only a foot and a half tall. By using models and miniatures, special effects artists can take viewers into new worlds of fantasy, horror, and adventure.

Stop-motion animation and miniatures

In 1933, RKO Studios produced a film that used every "gag" known at the time, including some spectacular uses of miniature figures that fooled audiences into thinking they were seeing the real thing. For a while, this film was known simply as Production 601. Then RKO decided to call the film *The Beast*. Later its name was changed to *The Eighth Wonder*. Before it was finished, however, the film was called by the name of its leading character, a name that would go down in movie history: *King Kong*.

The giant gorilla, King Kong, was the product of many different special effects, including traveling mattes and glass shots. Linwood Dunn used traveling mattes to show King Kong coming out of the jungle to claim a human sacrifice. The traveling mattes allowed the tiny model of Kong to appear in the same shot with a real human actor. Later in the film, Dunn used the same effect to show Kong climbing the side of New York's Empire State Building. For that scene, glass paintings of the New York City skyline were also used.

The real genius behind King Kong, however, was a model maker named Willis O'Brien. Although RKO sometimes claimed that its giant gorilla was forty feet tall, Kong was in fact a miniature, only eighteen inches high. Willis O'Brien designed King Kong and made him seem lifelike through a process called stop-motion animation.

As mentioned earlier, a movie camera takes twenty-four still pictures every second. When these still pictures are projected on a screen (again, at the rate of twenty-four per second), they seem to move. This illusion of movement is the basis for motion pictures.

Stop-motion animators take advantage of this illusion in much the same way that the makers of *The Execution of Mary Queen of Scots* did. Just as those early filmmakers stopped the camera to substitute a dummy for an actress, the stop-motion animator stops the camera over and over again to make small changes in his or her models and miniatures.

A painstaking process

For instance, to make King Kong walk through the jungle, Willis O'Brien took hundreds of pictures of the miniature gorilla. After each picture, O'Brien changed the position of Kong's legs and arms slightly. He slowly inched the model forward. When all the pictures were projected one after another, the model's arms and legs seemed to be moving—and King Kong looked like he was stomping through the jungle.

Using this method, it took O'Brien many days to complete just one fifteen-second shot. People at RKO said that O'Brien spent so much time with King Kong that the gorilla began to take on O'Brien's expressions and gestures.

During the making of *King Kong*, O'Brien built six different models of the gorilla, each eighteen inches high. Each model had a movable skeleton covered with rubber and rabbit fur. O'Brien also built tiny models of the snakes and dinosaurs that King Kong battled in the film.

Not all the shots of King Kong were miniatures. Producer Merian

C. Cooper ordered the RKO model makers to build a full-sized head for Kong. This head was eighteen feet high, big enough to hide several men inside. These men operated controls that moved Kong's mouth, lips, and neck. RKO claimed that the skins of eighty bears were used to provide hair for the giant model. The head was placed on a flat-car so that it could be moved easily about the set.

The giant head of King Kong allowed actress Fay Wray to play close-up shots. In these shots, the monster appeared to hold her right

Actress Jessica Lange screams at Kong's killers in the 1977 remake of King Kong. Advances in technology allowed the studio to use a more realistic, full-size model for the remake.

The mighty Kong swats at airplanes from atop his perch on a New York skyscraper in the 1933 version of King Kong. *Many special effects techniques were combined to make such scenes realistic.*

up to his face. In more distant scenes, however, Linwood Dunn sometimes used traveling mattes to add the actress to the shots. In other scenes, O'Brien replaced Wray with a six-inch miniature that looked just like her. This miniature is what Kong held in his hand as he "climbed" the Empire State Building.

While some scenes required Dunn's traveling mattes to place Kong in full-sized locations, other scenes were built entirely in miniature by O'Brien. To make his tiny jungles look believable, O'Brien employed two special effects tricks. He used glass paintings behind and in front of the scene to fill in trees, vines, and bushes. And he placed real human characters on his tiny sets by means of a system called rear projection.

Rear projection was first developed in the early 1930s as a way of bringing the outside world indoors. In the earliest motion pictures, actors had performed in front of painted scenery such as forests and castles. The actors looked like they were performing in a stage play. This did not always look believable. Filmmakers wanted to find a way to film actors on a studio stage—where it was easy to control lights, cameras, and sound recording equipment—and yet make it look like the actors really had been filmed outdoors. Rear projection was the solution.

Rear projection brings life to indoor scenes

With rear projection, a special movie screen is placed in back of the scene that is going to be filmed. Usually the actors stand or sit in front of this screen. A movie projector projects an image from behind the screen. The image shines through the screen, providing a background for the actors. This background might be a moving picture of a noisy street outside a cafe. Or it might be a shot of highway traffic speeding past an automobile—while an actor on stage pretends to be clinging to the roof of the car. Most often, rear projection is used to bring the *feel* of the outside world to a scene shot on an indoor stage.

Rear-projection scenes sometimes look slightly dark, because they are projected *through* a screen. For this reason, directors try to stage plenty of action in the front of the shot. Dramatic action helps distract viewers' attention away from a film's use of the rear-projection special effect.

Willis O'Brien came up with the idea of using rear projection to add actors to some of his shots. Moving pictures of the actors were projected onto rear-projection screens. Then actions, such as King Kong battling a dinosaur, were staged in front of the screens. This made it look as if the actors were in the background while Kong was walking around or fighting the dinosaur. Since O'Brien was shooting tiny models of King Kong, the dinosaur, and other monsters on very small sets, he had to use very small rear-projection screens. That way his actors would also look small and would fit right into the scenes.

The small rear-projection screens worked to O'Brien's advantage in another way. The light on the smaller screens was more concentrated than on a big screen. That meant that O'Brien's rear-projected figures were brighter than normal rear-projection images. They really looked like they were part of the action.

The special effects crew at Industrial Light and Magic used this same technique when they filmed *Return of the Jedi*. For the celebration in the Ewok Village, twelve rear-projection screens were set up. The screens were used to add a dozen groups of the tiny, bearlike Ewoks to different parts of the village scene.

Courtesy of Boss Film Corporation

A sculptor creates a clay model of Terror Dog for the movie Ghostbusters. *The model will be used to make a latex stop-motion puppet. The artist's creation will then be brought to life through special effects magic.*

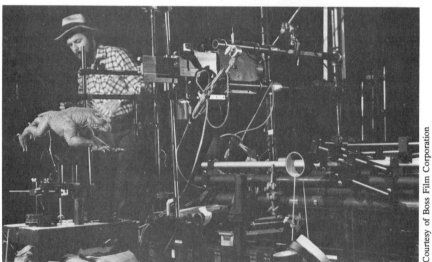

The Ghostbusters' *Terror Dog has a movable metal skeleton. When covered with foam rubber and latex skin, Terror Dog can be moved and filmed by the stop-motion camera to create a lifelike monster.*

The special effects in *King Kong* took more than a year to photograph. For a while, the producers at RKO feared the studio would go bankrupt before the film was finished. But *King Kong* was a smash hit at the box office and restored the studio's fortunes.

Over the years, many filmmakers have copied the techniques first used so effectively in the original *King Kong*. With the coming of World War II, studio special effects departments used their skill in photographing miniatures to re-create military battles. Dozens of miniature ships were blown up in studio water tanks.

Today it is easy to spot these scenes. That is because special effects artists never figured out how to make small waves, filmed in a studio tank, look like the giant waves of the ocean. When the small waves crashed against a model ship, they sent out drops of water— and drops of water always looked like drops of water. A miniature ship might have looked completely convincing, but as soon as a wave broke over it, the ship looked like a toy in a bathtub.

A model of the aircraft carrier Invincible *blazes in the movie* Ships With Wings. *Miniature planes and soldiers complete the scene. Many such models and miniatures have to be destroyed by fire and explosions in war movies to make scenes look real.*

After the war, stop-motion animator Ray Harryhausen used Willis O'Brien's techniques to bring new monsters to life. Harryhausen learned the art of stop-motion animation from O'Brien when the two of them worked on *Mighty Joe Young* in 1949. Joe Young looked like a "small" King Kong—this time the gorilla was only supposed to be twelve feet tall. Once again, miniatures were photographed in such a way as to make the gorilla look large and powerful. Twenty-six special effects craftspeople spent three years creating Mighty Joe Young.

In *The Beast from 20,000 Fathoms* (1953), Harryhausen used mattes and miniatures to show a dinosaur invading New York City. Japanese

The Greek hero Jason battles an army of skeletons in Jason and the Argonauts. *Each movement made by the skeletons had to be filmed with a stop-action camera. One half second of screen time took a full day's filming!*

filmmakers also used models and stop-motion animation to create the monster Godzilla, who destroyed many tiny cities in films of the 1950s and 1960s. The special effects experts at Walt Disney Studios photographed miniatures under water, then built a full-sized giant squid to battle a submarine in *Twenty Thousand Leagues Under the Sea* (1956).

Harryhausen often turned to fairy tales and myths to provide subjects for his special effects. The hero of *Jason and the Argonauts* (1963) battled seven skeletons swinging swords and spears, all of them moving at the same time. The skeletons were models, and each had to be readjusted many times just to photograph a single sword swing. This scene was so complex that it took Harryhausen a full day to shoot only twelve frames (or still pictures)—adding up to one-half second of screen time.

Harryhausen continued making films into the *Star Wars* era. His tiny monsters looked less believable, however, when they were compared to the work of a new generation of special effects animators at companies like Industrial Light and Magic.

CHAPTER SIX

Good Monsters Need Good Stories

ILM's Jon Berg first saw *Mighty Joe Young* when he was four years old. Berg was terrified, and he spent most of the film holding his hands over his eyes. That experience stuck with him as he grew older. It taught him that films work best when they combine believable effects with powerful stories.

Stop-motion animation at ILM

As a teenager, Berg was inspired by his memory of *Mighty Joe Young* to build rubber puppets and to study stop-motion animation. After college, Berg went to work for Cascade Studios, a Los Angeles company that made commercials for television. Berg animated models of the Pillsbury Doughboy and Speedy Alka-Seltzer and animated the hands and feet of the Jolly Green Giant.

At Cascade, Berg became friends with Dennis Muren. Muren later invited the young stop-motion animator to work with him at Industrial Light and Magic. There Berg designed the living chess pieces that were used by the characters Chewbacca and R2D2 in *Star Wars*. This special effect was on-screen for only a short time, but it helped establish Chewy and R2D2 as funny, sympathetic characters.

One way in which the *Star Wars* films grab audiences' attention is by opening in the middle of things. Right from the opening moments, the films deliver exciting stories combined with spectacular special effects. For the opening scene in *The Empire Strikes Back* (1980), Jon Berg built the imperial snowwalkers that attacked Luke Skywalker and his army. These monsterlike fortresses look like giant metal animals. They move across the snow on mechanical legs, spitting laser blasts at the attacking rebel troops. In reality, however, the snowwalkers were eighteen-inch-tall stop-motion miniatures.

Snowwalkers based on an elephant's walk

To correctly capture the awkward, rolling walk of these giant machines, Berg and the ILM crew came up with a unique idea. They borrowed an elephant and paraded it around the company parking lot to study the way it walked. Then they tried to imitate the elephant's movement when they animated the movement of the snowwalkers.

The miniature snowwalkers were photographed in the middle of a large room covered with artificial snow. Each time the crew needed to change the position of one of the snowwalkers—which was hundreds of times—they had to figure out how to get to the model without leaving tracks in the snowfield. Workers often had to hang above the miniature set on platforms that looked like diving boards, just so they could reach the models.

For the snowwalker scene, the special effects camera crew also had to shine lights on the fake snow so that it matched real-life scenes shot in the snowfields of Norway. The ILM crew's skill in blending this scene's live-action shots with miniatures—in one case using traveling mattes to send Luke Skywalker flying between the legs of an imperial snowwalker—make *Empire*'s use of stop-motion miniatures difficult for audiences to spot. Since the spectacular action looks so real, audiences are caught up in the fear and excitement experienced by Luke and his friends.

Industrial Light and Magic has used stop-motion animation on many recent films. The company's aim has been to make its special effects more believable, even while they seem more and more im-

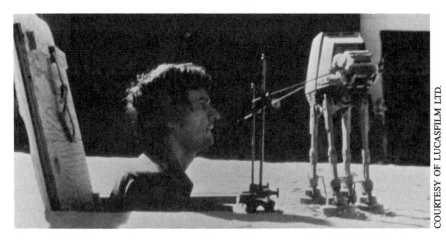

A special-effects artist moves an imperial snowwalker in The Empire Strikes Back. *The snowwalker models had to be moved hundreds of times in order to make them look as if they were walking across the movie screen.*

possible. The nightmarish skeleton in the closet in *Poltergeist* (1982) is a model filmed by stop-motion animation. The model was filmed inside a tank of water. This made the model's hair rise up, so that the skeleton appears to be floating in the air. The shot was later added to the matted-out section of a shot of a child's closet.

The ILM "go-motion" technique

The flying dragon in *Dragonslayer* (1981) received special treatment from the ILM crew. For this film, the animators discovered a way to make a model dragon's stop-motion movement look even more realistic. They called their new technique go-motion.

Stop-motion figures in the films of Willis O'Brien and Ray Harryhausen always looked a little jerky. The figures' movements had a stop-start quality that looked unreal, particularly to more sophisticated audiences who were used to smooth, invisible special effects.

This jerky movement was caused by the stop-motion technique used by O'Brien and Harryhausen. In stop-motion animation, each point in a model's movement is filmed by the camera while the model is at rest. King Kong's foot was raised slightly, then a picture was taken. The foot was raised a little higher, and another picture was taken. Eventually the film showed King Kong taking a giant step, but his movement did not look entirely real. It still had a slight stop-start quality to it.

If King Kong were really alive, his foot would be moving each time the camera took a picture of it. Even at the rate of twenty-four pictures a second, the camera could not help but film a slightly blurred image of the figure in motion. It is this slight "blur" that is missing from stop-motion animation—and that was added to ILM films by the go-motion process.

For the go-motion animation in *Dragonslayer*, the special effects crew at ILM attached blue rods to parts of the dragon's body. (The rods were colored blue so they would not show up on the special kind of movie film that was used.) These rods were connected to a motor, whose movement was programmed by a computer. When the motor turned, the rods moved the dragon's wings, jaws, and body—and the camera captured this motion. The model's movement still had to be filmed in many separate stages, but now each stage looked more lifelike because it had a slightly blurred quality on film. The same technique was used to create the movements of the two-headed dragon in *Willow*.

The importance of good stories

Go-motion was a real step forward in the art of special effects, but special effects alone do not determine a film's success. *Dragonslayer*'s story did not capture viewers' emotions the way the filmmakers hoped it would. The film *E.T.: The Extra-Terrestrial* (1982), on the other hand, succeeded in spite of some weak special effects.

Although *E.T.* contains some wonderful "gags" like E.T. and Elliot flying across the sky on Elliot's bicycle (created through a traveling matte), the character E.T. himself is not entirely convincing. In many scenes he looks like a big rubber doll. What makes *E.T.* so popular with audiences is the story the film tells. Audiences around the world have responded to Melissa Mathison's script about a lonely, frightened character trying desperately to get home. As one special effects expert put it, "With a script like that, you could cast E.T. as a guy with a paper bag over his head and it would still work."

By contrast, the most expensive monster movie ever made was a giant flop. In 1977, a Hollywood studio remade *King Kong*, using a remarkable forty-foot-high mechanical monster. Twenty special effects technicians were needed to operate this giant gorilla. But the story of the mighty gorilla no longer stirred people's emotions.

Elliot and E.T. fly through the night sky in the movie E.T. *Brilliant special effects and a heart-warming story made* E.T. *one of the biggest movie hits in history.*

Actress Jessica Lange sits in the hand of the new Kong in the 1977 remake. Twenty special effects technicians were needed to operate Kong.

Viewers were more interested in how much money it had cost to build and photograph the big ape. (One estimate was $24 million.)

Industrial Light and Magic has had its share of flops, too. The film *Howard the Duck* (1986) was filled with explosions, horrible monsters, clever miniatures, and beautiful matte paintings. But audiences did not respond to the film's leading character, a fast-talking duck from outer space. *Howard the Duck* seemed like an attempt to remake the story of *E.T.* But Howard lacked the gentle, childlike innocence that has made the little space traveler in *E.T.* so popular. As a result, producer George Lucas lost millions of dollars on *Howard the Duck*.

Special effects need good stories

Special effects by themselves are almost never enough to make a movie successful. Popular special effects movies like *E.T.* and *Star Wars* have succeeded because their stories and characters remind audiences of the fun and fear of childhood adventures.

Few films ever excited, scared, and thrilled audiences the way the original *King Kong* did. This was partly because the film's special effects were new to audiences in 1933. No one had ever seen anything like *King Kong*.

But *King Kong* also touched people's deeper feelings. In 1933, America was entering the fourth year of the Great Depression. Millions of people were out of work. Bank closings caused many people to lose their life's savings. The whole country felt frightened, confused, and frustrated.

Americans in 1933 knew how it felt to have once been powerful and now to feel chained and helpless. When audiences saw King Kong breaking free of his chains and stomping across New York City, they cheered for him. Kong stirred people's buried memories of pride and power and freedom. Through the art of special effects, the makers of the original *King Kong* were able to portray the fears and dreams of a troubled nation.

CHAPTER SEVEN

The 700-Layer Cake

Ridley Scott, the director of *Blade Runner* and *Alien*, once said, "To me, a film is like a 700-layer cake." Scott meant that a film—particularly a film that uses special effects—is built up by adding more and more effects to each scene. Scott often asks his special effects crew to combine many effects that have been shot separately. Layered together, these effects form one "impossible" scene: a scene that looks like it was filmed all at one time.

Blade Runner, for instance, opens with a scene in which the camera passes over the landscape of Los Angeles as it might look in the year 2019. Scott's crew called this scene "Ridley's inferno" because it looks like a nightmare vision of the future.

"Ridley's inferno" was built up of many layers. First, a model of the city was built on a table top. On-screen, the model looked like it stretched for miles, but it was really only eighteen-feet wide. Next, electricians set up more than 2,000 lights to shine from within the model. Flames from smokestacks were filmed separately and projected onto the scene by a technique similar to rear projection.

Smoky air was also filmed separately and added to this opening scene of *Blade Runner*. The air seemed to cover the model city. Huge buildings rising above the city—they actually were just large photographs of other model buildings—were positioned in the background. Finally, a flying car (a miniature, of course) was filmed passing over the landscape. To capture all these elements on film, the camera had to photograph the same scene many different times.

When special effects workers put together all the different layers of a scene like "Ridley's inferno" or a *Star Wars* battle, they use two important tools: the optical printer and the motion-control camera. The optical printer combines images—moving pictures—that have been filmed at different times and places. It also permits filmmakers to make changes within those images. The motion-control camera allows filmmakers to shoot the same scene, in exactly the same way, over and over again, adding new elements as they go along.

Optical printers

The man who first taught Hollywood filmmakers how to use the optical printer was Linwood Dunn, special effects designer for *King Kong* and *Citizen Kane*. In 1928, Dunn was looking for work. He had worked as a Hollywood cameraman for two years, but now the only job he could find was playing part-time in a dance band. One day Dunn got a call from the camera operators' union. A new studio, RKO, needed a cameraman to work for a few days on a special matte shot. Dunn took the job, not knowing it would launch him on a fifty-year career.

The RKO studio liked Dunn's work. Soon he was employed full-time as a cameraman in the special effects department. "I really lucked out," Dunn says. "The big studios like Fox and Metro had a separate department for everything—one for matte paintings, one for optical printing, one specially for miniatures, another for background projection—but at RKO everything came through the one department."

Dunn was able to study all the different kinds of special effects techniques. His main interest, however, soon became the optical printer, and he became known as Hollywood's master of the machine. He twice received Hollywood's highest honor, the Academy Award, for developing better optical printers.

An optical printer basically is a movie projector that is set up facing a camera. This projector sends an image that has already been filmed

Oscar-winning special effects master Linwood Dunn.

onto a fresh strip of film in the camera. This allows the camera to film the image a second time. (In other words, the camera takes a picture of a picture.) During this second filming, the camera can be set to run fast or slow, making the action appear slowed down or sped up. If the camera is moved closer to the projector, it will record only part of the image, making that part look bigger on-screen.

Tricks like split screens, traveling mattes, ''frozen'' (still) images, and *wipes* (where one image seems to push another off the screen) are handled easily by optical printers. In these and other ways, optical printers are used to combine the many separate layers of complex special effects shots.

Motion-control camera systems

Filmmakers often like to move their camera while they are filming. Many times the camera will tilt up or down, move in or out, pan left or right, or change focus (how clearly objects can be seen in the distance) to follow the action of a scene. If a scene needs to be filmed several times in order to ''layer in'' special effects (like the opening scene in *Blade Runner*), camera movement can create problems.

It is almost impossible for camera operators to repeat a camera movement in exactly the same way unless they have special equipment to help them. For this reason, special effects technicians developed computer systems that could remember camera movements and repeat them exactly. A computer-guided moving camera is called a motion-control camera system.

Motion-control systems

The first modern motion-control system was devised for the filming of the space adventure *2001*. This film combined elegant camera movement with believable-looking models and special effects.

The effects crew on *2001* did not have a computer to program repeatable movements for their camera. By using mechanical gears and levers, however, they were able to repeat certain camera movements very precisely. This enabled them to layer elements into a scene. The crew shot many different objects for a single scene—stars, spaceships, space stations—and each time they used the same

A one-man space pod leaves its mother ship the Discovery *to explore space in* 2001: A Space Odyssey. *Stanley Kubrick's special effects masterpiece was made without the aid of computer-controlled cameras.*

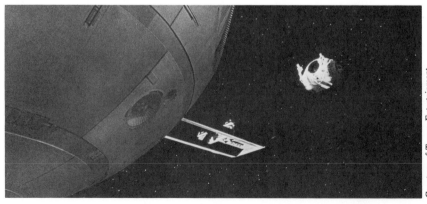

Courtesy of Turner Entertainment

camera movement. They then combined all the objects into one shot in the optical printer. Their work was so successful that George Lucas says *2001* is still the movie against which all other special effects movies must be measured.

In one scene in *2001*, an astronaut goes on a wild ride through a tunnel of lights. This "stargate corridor" was created by special effects designer Douglas Trumbull. Trumbull used the motion-control system to make the camera duplicate the same movement over and over again. Each time the camera moved down the corridor, different colors and light effects were added to the scene—but the camera movement was always the same. Sometimes, however, Trumbull made the camera move slower or faster. This variation in speed caused the passing lights to have a "streaking" effect—as if each light source was pulling a tail of light behind it.

Trumbull later used this streaking effect when he designed television commercials and new logos for television networks. For the ABC

The optical printer combines images filmed at different times and places. It allows filmmakers to create complex effects by layering photos of different objects.

logo, Trumbull made the letters "ABC" rush towards the camera, with each letter leaving a trail of light behind it.

After finishing *2001*, Trumbull designed new motion-control systems that used computers to "remember" the camera's changes in movement and focus. For Steven Spielberg's *Close Encounters of the Third Kind*, Trumbull and his father Don (who had worked on *The Wizard of Oz* forty years earlier) built a computerized camera system that they called the "icebox." In the same way that people use a refrigerator to store food, the Trumbulls used the icebox computer to store information—information about scenes that had been shot with a moving camera.

One example of a motion-control scene in *Close Encounters of the Third Kind* involved a shot of the night sky. (Actually, the shot was a painting of the night sky. *Close Encounters* used one hundred matte paintings.) This "sky" was filmed with the camera moving, and the motion-control computer—the icebox—was programmed to remember how the camera moved.

Adding miniatures to the scene

Later, the information stored in the icebox was recalled, and the same camera movements used in filming the night sky were repeated while the camera filmed the Indiana landscape (which was actually a model). On this second filming, the camera was run at a slower speed, taking just one picture at a time. This slower camera speed enabled the special effects crew to add miniatures to the scene and to make the miniatures move through stop-motion animation.

In the final version of this scene from *Close Encounters*, the effects crew layered in another shot of spaceships passing over the Indiana landscape. Again, the spaceship scene had been shot with a motion-control camera. The fields, roads, trucks, and telephone poles in this scene were all miniatures; the spaceships were models; and the sky was a painting. Through motion-control photography, these moving-camera shots of the night sky, the spaceships, and the miniature landscape were filmed separately, then blended to look like a single scene.

In 1975, Douglas Trumbull was approached by a young director named George Lucas, who was preparing to make a film called *Star Wars*. Lucas needed someone who could put together a special effects crew, assemble the necessary cameras and equipment, and shoot 365 complicated special effects shots.

To create those 365 shots, nearly 4,000 images would have to be filmed and then layered together, one image on top of another. Shots of space battles, for instance, might involve dozens of separate shots of starfighters, laser blasts, asteroids, matte paintings, and so forth. Each of these elements had to be filmed separately, then combined to produce the final image.

Dykstra and Lucas work together

The man Trumbull recommended to Lucas for *Star Wars* was John Dykstra. Dykstra had been a pilot, motorcycle racer, and race car driver. He is a huge man—six feet, four inches tall—with long hair, a thick beard, and a booming voice. By contrast, Lucas is a short, soft-spoken man who more than once has been mistaken for the ILM office boy. Dykstra and Lucas admired each other's filmmaking skills, but their relationship quickly became a stormy one.

As the first head of Industrial Light and Magic, John Dykstra put together a loyal team made up of old friends and students just out of art school. Over the next several months, Dykstra counted on his crew's loyalty to see him through several small "wars" with their boss, George Lucas. Dykstra had learned from Douglas Trumbull that a special effects supervisor has "creative rights": he has the right to insist that special effects be done properly, even if that brings him into conflict with his director. As a result of this attitude, Dykstra and Lucas butted heads many times during the making of *Star Wars*.

At the beginning of the *Star Wars* shoot, Lucas showed Dykstra a reel of black-and-white film that he had spliced together from old combat movies. He told Dykstra that he wanted the space battles in *Star Wars* to look like these aerial "dogfights" fought by combat planes in World War II. That meant that Dykstra would have to design a motion-control camera that could move freely in any direction, in order to duplicate the planes' movement.

Dykstra and his crew designed just such a camera, controlled by computers. It worked beautifully. In fact, in the final version of *Star Wars*, none of the model spaceships actually move. The illusion that the spaceships are moving was created by Dykstra's moving camera.

Dykstra sometimes argued, however, that Lucas was trying too hard to imitate the images in his World War II dogfight movies. Dykstra came up with different ways to film the space battle scenes. Lucas did not like them. Each man had his own vision of how the film should be made, and neither one wanted to back off. "Like anyone with the guts to become a director and tackle something like *Star Wars*," Dykstra said of Lucas, "his tendency was to want to do everything himself."

Director and film genius George Lucas is best-known for the Star Wars *films.*

Lucas worried that Dykstra was spending too much time building the motion-control system. After more than a year's work, ILM had spent over a million dollars (half the film's effects budget) and produced only three shots. All of Dykstra's efforts seemed to be going into producing the complicated motion-control system. Lucas felt the job could be done more simply.

The relationship deteriorates

One day, Lucas lost his temper and began yelling at Dykstra. Dykstra yelled back. After that, the two men harbored bitter feelings toward each other. Only later, after Dykstra's camera was fully operational, did Lucas realize how much time and effort the system could save in creating special effects shots.

Dykstra's motion-control camera system allowed the ILM crew to return to space battles they had shot weeks before and add new elements like laser blasts or explosions. At first the crew jokingly called this camera "the Dykstraflex." But with the success of *Star Wars* the Dykstraflex camera became known as one of the best motion-control systems in the film industry. The Dykstraflex system allows filmmakers to repeat complicated camera movements long after an original shot has been filmed.

When *Star Wars* was finished, Dykstra left Industrial Light and Magic. He went to Hawaii for a month, thinking that he would have to look for a new job when he came back to California. While he was gone, *Star Wars* became a blockbuster hit.

On the strength of *Star Wars*'s special effects—and the brilliant motion-control system that Dykstra had designed—he was able to open his own company, which he called Apogee. Today Apogee and Douglas Trumbull's company EEG (Entertainment Effects Group) are two of the most widely respected special effects companies in the film industry.

CHAPTER EIGHT

Having a Blast

Not all special effects involve camera tricks. When filmmakers want to blow up villages, set tall office buildings on fire, or gun down gangsters with machine guns, they often ask their special effects crews to create physical effects. Physical effects are special effects that actually take place in front of the camera. Fires, gunshots, and explosions are some of the most common kinds of physical effects. They add great excitement to films—but they can also be dangerous.

Gunshots

As late as 1935, filmmakers used live bullets to give audiences the feeling that they were watching deadly gun battles. In the 1935 film *G-Men*, the actor James Cagney stood in a window while the frame around him was ripped apart by bullets. The bullets were real ones, fired from just offscreen by an expert marksman.

Hollywood's special effects artists eventually developed a safer way to imitate gunshots. When a scene called for bullets to strike the side of a building, the special effects crew drilled small holes in the wall. The crew then pushed tiny explosive charges, called squibs, into these holes. The squibs contained just enough gunpowder to create a believable-looking explosion.

Detonation wires were attached to the squibs, so that the gunpowder charges inside them could be set off from a distance. Finally, the holes were plugged with putty or wax and painted over. When the squibs were set off during filming, the wall looked like it was being struck by bullets.

Films like *Bonnie and Clyde* and *The Godfather* used a similar technique to show bullets striking human beings. When the Godfather's oldest son, played by James Caan, was gunned down at a highway toll booth, it looked like bullets were striking his arms, legs, and chest. To create this illusion, the special effects crew first taped small metal plates all over Caan's body. They then fastened squibs to the metal plates. The plates protected the actor's skin when the squibs exploded. Small plastic envelopes filled with fake blood were placed on top of the squibs.

Caan's costume hid the squibs, as well as the wires used to set them off. These wires ran down Caan's body and out through his pants leg. A special effects technician operated a control panel that set off the charges in the proper order. As the charges exploded, the actor jerked and twisted his body. The squibs ripped holes in Caan's clothes, and fake blood went flying everywhere. The whole effect was gruesome and very believable.

Fires

Setting actors on fire is one of the most dangerous kinds of special effects. In *The Towering Inferno*, actress Susan Flannery played a character trapped in a burning building. Trying to escape the flames, the character catches fire and is sucked out of a high window by a rush of air.

To handle this difficult scene, the filmmakers substituted a stuntman for the actress. Stuntmen (and a few stuntwomen) are actors who are paid to perform dangerous and difficult tricks (''stunts'') in place of a film's actual stars. Their work often goes unnoticed by audiences because the switch from star to stuntperson usually takes place at the last moment—right before a character falls off a building, catches fire, or crashes in a speeding automobile.

In *The Towering Inferno*, the stuntman doubling for Susan Flannery had to wear several layers of protective clothing. Next to his skin he wore long, fireproof underwear. Over this he wore a "silver suit," the same kind of aluminum-based fire protection worn by race car drivers. The stuntman's outer clothes were made of flame-resistant material, and he wore asbestos gloves. To protect his face, he wore a flame-proof mask (like a ski mask) underneath a mask that had been molded to look like Susan Flannery's face.

A stuntman falls down a stairwell shattered by an explosion in The Towering Inferno. *The physical special effects called for in disaster movies can be very dangerous. Trained stuntpeople are substituted for actors in these movies.*

Courtesy of Twentieth Century-Fox Film Corporation

The special effects crew on *The Towering Inferno* coated the stuntman's back with a flammable paste. This paste produced a "cold fire," flames that burned brightly without giving off too much heat. As the stuntman took his flaming leap, the camera crew knew that they had only twenty seconds to record the shot. After that, other stuntmen would rush in and extinguish the fire, whether the scene was over or not.

The top stuntpeople prefer to have other stuntpeople, rather than firefighters, handle the fire extinguishers. They say that only someone who has been lit on fire himself can appreciate the danger of the situation. After twenty seconds, both the flames and the lack of breathing air pose real threats to the burning stuntperson's safety.

Setting buildings ablaze

Setting buildings on fire is usually safer than setting people on fire. In both cases, however, the special effects crew has to make the fire look believable. For *The Towering Inferno*, nearly sixty full-sized sets were built to look like rooms in a burning building. Gas pipes hidden all around the sets could be turned on and off to control the size of flames used in each shot.

A seventy-foot-high model was used for shots of the burning building itself. This model had to be large, because fire, like water, is hard to miniaturize. If a model is too small, flames will look too big for the building. Special effects crews sometimes have to line up flames at a distance behind a model, so that the flames will look smaller and match the size of the model.

For the burning of the city of Atlanta in *Gone with the Wind*, full-sized sets were used. The fire was one of the biggest in the history of Hollywood, and hundreds of stars dropped by to watch the scene being filmed. Part of the blaze was created by burning the giant wall that had been constructed five years earlier as a set for *King Kong*.

Movie explosions are even more dangerous than fires. Explosions often send building parts, trees, and perhaps even stuntpeople, flying

The city of Atlanta burns during a scene from the 1939 movie Gone with the Wind. *The fire was the largest ever staged by Hollywood filmmakers. Because the scene could be filmed only once, it had to be done right the first time.*

through the air. Effects crews have to make sure that actors, camera operators, and camera equipment are all safely shielded from a blast.

For special effects explosions, either models or full-sized sets can be used. When a model is blown up, small charges similar to squibs are used. Often the model is "preweakened"; that is, parts of it are sawn through so that the structure will collapse easily when the charges explode. With larger buildings, walls are sometimes pulled out with piano wire just at the moment of explosion. This helps the building collapse and helps keep a safe limit on the size of the explosion needed to bring down the building.

Besides being dangerous, movie explosions can also be costly. Film-makers sometimes want to blow up expensive airplanes or helicopters to create dazzling special effects. At Industrial Light and Magic, models are usually substituted for real airplanes or helicopters before explosions take place. In the old television series *Mission Impossible*, helicopters always disappeared behind a hill or a tall building before

Explosions from the 1942 movie Ships with Wings. *Such explosions must look realistic and yet be controlled enough to be safe.*

they "exploded." Audiences saw a huge ball of flame coming from the spot where the helicopter had disappeared—but the flame was just burning gasoline. The expensive helicopter had been saved to use in filming other episodes.

Hollywood filmmakers recently have had to reconsider the ways in which they use special effects explosions. At two o'clock in the morning on July 23, 1982, a terrible accident took place on the set of *Twilight Zone: The Motion Picture.* The film's crew was working late, trying to complete one last shot. The shot was supposed to look like a battle scene from the Vietnam War. In the film's story, a character played by Vic Morrow was supposed to save the lives of two Vietnamese children by carrying them across a river. A helicopter would be shooting at them while the children's village blew up in the background.

Director John Landis wanted the shot to look perfect. The "Vietnamese village," which the crew had built on a river north of Los Angeles, would actually be destroyed by special effects explosions. Since the village could only be blown up once, six cameras would be used at the same time to record many different shots of the scene.

Landis gave the signal for the action to begin. As buildings exploded all around him, Morrow picked up the two child actors and carried them into the river. The giant helicopter circled overhead, its forty-four-foot blade creating a tremendous rush of wind.

Director Landis wanted the scene to look real. "Lower! Lower! Lower!" he shouted to the helicopter pilot. "Fire! Fire! Fire!" Suddenly, one of the special effects explosions on the ground shook the big chopper. The pilot struggled to keep the helicopter aloft, but it went out of control and fell into the river. It landed right on top of Morrow and the two children. The helicopter's blade was still spinning wildly as it crashed.

On the banks of the river, everyone stood frozen in disbelief. For a moment, the crew thought that the helicopter crash might be just one more special effect. But Landis and several crew members quickly realized what had happened. They rushed into the river to rescue the actors, but it was too late. The crashing helicopter had taken the lives of Vic Morrow, six-year-old Renee Shinn Chin, and seven-year-old Myca Dinh Le.

The *Twilight Zone* accident caused a furor in Hollywood. In recent years, filmmakers had tried harder and harder to create "impossible" effects. Sometimes they had taken great risks to make these effects believable. Now people were asking whether the risks had been worth it.

The County of Los Angeles charged John Landis with criminal neglect. Landis, it was charged, had risked the lives of Morrow and the child actors by placing them in a scene that was far too dangerous. After a long trial, the director was found not guilty. His studio, however, had to pay huge sums to the families of the actors who had been killed.

Nine months after the *Twilight Zone* crash, director Steven Spielberg (who also worked on *Twilight Zone*) spoke to the press. "No movie is worth dying for," Spielberg said. "If something isn't safe, it's the right and responsibility of every actor and crew member to yell, 'Cut!'"

CHAPTER NINE

Growing Old and Going Ape

When movie actors turn into werewolves, apes, or monsters, they often do so through the magic of effects makeup. This branch of special effects has become increasingly important over the last twenty years. From the deformed face of the Elephant Man to the stabbed, chopped, and chainsawed victims in movies like *Friday the 13th*, the use of effects makeup has become more and more believable.

Movie actors almost always wear some kind of makeup. That is because bright lights are used in filmmaking. Without makeup, the lights would make the actors' faces look shiny or rough on-screen.

Actors also use pastes, powders, and wigs to make themselves look older or younger. Effects makeup goes beyond these traditional functions of movie makeup. Effects makeup makes actors look very different from their actual appearances.

Early effects makeup

The first movie actor to rely heavily on effects makeup was the silent screen star Lon Chaney. Chaney was known as "the man of a thousand faces." For roles like *The Phantom of the Opera* (1925), Chaney used loops of wire to stretch open his eyelids, mouth, and nostrils. The gaping holes produced by the wire loops gave Chaney's face a terrifying appearance.

Effects makeup enabled Chaney to play many scary roles, including an apeman, a murderous old woman, and the Hunchback of Notre Dame. A popular joke in the 1920s went, "Don't step on that spider, it might be Lon Chaney."

For the movie *Frankenstein* (1931), actor Boris Karloff was cast as a monster whom a mad scientist had assembled from pieces of dead bodies. Makeup artist Jack Pierce studied books on surgery to decide how the monster should look. He wanted Karloff to look as if a brain had been planted in his head. "I decided to make the monster's head square and flat, like a box," Pierce said, "and dig that big scar across the forehead and have metal clamps hold it together." Pierce also gave Karloff metal studs on each side of his neck. These were the connection points through which the monster could be jolted to life by an electrical charge.

Pierce's makeup extended from the top of Karloff's head down to the actor's eyelids. The rest of Karloff's face was left uncovered. This permitted the actor to express a wide range of emotions, from surprise to delight to anger. The combination of Karloff's acting talents and Jack Pierce's clever effects makeup made the Frankenstein monster one of the most popular movie monsters of all time.

Creating a werewolf

Lon Chaney's son, Lon Chaney Jr., played another famous movie monster in the 1940 film *The Wolf Man*. Audiences were treated to the sight of Chaney's face and hands sprouting fur right before their eyes, when the full moon turned Chaney's character into a werewolf.

Chaney's on-screen transformation into a werewolf was accomplished by Jack Pierce. Pierce used yak hair and greasepaint to construct Chaney's hairy features. He then employed a technique used in stop-motion animation, the procedure that filmmakers use to make miniature figures move. As Pierce built up Chaney's effects makeup little by little, he turned the camera on and off many times, taking many separate pictures of the gradual change in the Wolf Man's

Lon Chaney Sr. was the first movie actor to use elaborate special effects makeup. One of his most frightening characters was the Phantom from the 1925 movie Phantom of the Opera.

appearance. When the sequence was shown on-screen, Chaney's transformation into a werewolf seemed to happen smoothly in a matter of seconds.

Latex

Although Hollywood continued to create movie monsters over the years, the greatest advances in effects makeup took place during the 1970s. During this time, special effects artists found many new uses for latex.

Latex is a liquid rubber that can be applied in thin layers to change actors' appearances. Effects artists use latex to make actors look

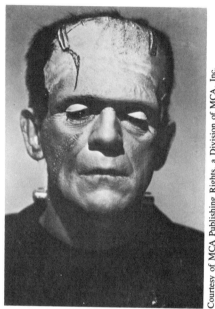

Frankenstein, one of Hollywood's most famous monsters, was brought to life by makeup artist Jack Pierce and actor Boris Karloff.

wrinkled as their characters grow older. In the film *Little Big Man* (1970), actor Dustin Hoffman aged from a teenager to a 121-year-old man. As the character grew older and older, Hoffman had to wear more and more makeup. By the end of the film, he was wearing several pounds of latex on his face.

Makeup artist Dick Smith used the same technique a dozen years later to turn rock star David Bowie into a 150-year-old ex-vampire in *The Hunger* (1983). On the other hand, just a few thin layers of latex helped Smith turn an older actor, Marlon Brando, into a believable-looking old man for his role in *The Godfather* (1972).

Latex can be used to fashion whole new faces and body parts for characters whose appearance is not entirely human. To make a mask for an actor, the effects artist first makes a mold of the actor's face. To do this, the artist covers the actor's face with latex while the actor breathes through straws in his or her nostrils. The latex hardens into a mold that captures the actor's features. This mold can then be used to make a mask that looks just like the actor. It also provides a basis for adding new features to the actor's appearance. For instance, Mr. Spock's pointed ears in *Star Trek* were made from a mold of actor Leonard Nimoy's own ears. From this starting point, the latex ears were stretched and shaped to look like Spock's ears.

In the 1968 film *Planet of the Apes*, actors were turned into apes by special effects artist John Chambers. Chambers used separate pieces of latex to cover each actor's forehead, upper lip, and lower lip. The resulting three-part latex masks allowed the actors to move their facial muscles normally. Thin layers of latex makeup were used to fill in the spaces between the more prominent ape features. The actors were able to speak and show normal human emotions even though their faces were hidden beneath rubber ape masks.

One problem with the latex masks used in *Planet of the Apes* was that they could be worn only once, since they tore each time they

The magic of latex allowed makeup artist John Chambers to create the memorable ape-like inhabitants of Earth's future in Planet of the Apes.

were removed. As a result, Chambers had to make many copies of each actor's rubber face pieces. Makeup artist Werner Keppler had the same problem with the pointed ears worn by Leonard Nimoy when he played Mr. Spock in *Star Trek II: The Wrath of Khan* (1982). Since the ears tore when Nimoy took them off, Keppler had to prepare a new set of ears for each day's filming. "I had only one mold," Keppler said, "and every night after shooting I had to go home and make the next day's ears." Keppler cooked Spock's latex ears for several hours in his kitchen stove, baking them every night until one in the morning.

Dick Smith and *The Exorcist*

Makeup artist Dick Smith created some of the most memorable effects makeup in recent films. In addition to aging the stars of *Little Big Man*, *The Godfather*, and *The Hunger*, Smith made actor William Hurt's face seem to melt in *Altered States* (1980), and he blew up an actor's head in *Scanners* (1981).

Smith's most famous special effects were crafted for the 1973 film *The Exorcist*. This film tells the story of a little girl whose body is taken over by the devil. In one scene, the girl's head turns 360 degrees. In another scene she vomits huge amounts of green slime, and in still another scene the words "Help Me" appear in blisters on her stomach.

Actress Linda Blair was cast as the girl in *The Exorcist*. In addition to wearing makeup that made her face look pale and bruised, Blair wore special contact lenses that made her eyes look yellow. These lenses caused Blair great discomfort, but they made her character look even more inhuman.

For the head-turning scene, Dick Smith made a fiberglass dummy of Blair's body and a separate, lifelike model of her head. In the film, it was the dummy's head that audiences saw turning all the way around. The head was equipped with radio-controlled eyes whose blinking made the effect seem even more believable.

For the vomiting scene, narrow tubes were attached to the side of Blair's face. The tubes were covered with makeup so that they could not be seen by viewers. Offscreen, two men pumped a mixture of pea soup and oatmeal through the tubes, creating the green glop that seemed to be coming out of Blair's mouth.

To make the words "Help Me" appear on Blair's stomach, Smith made a latex mold of her torso. He used cleaning fluid to paint the words "Help Me" onto this fake stomach. The cleaning fluid caused the latex to blister in the shape of the desired letters. When the cleaning fluid was heated with hot air from a hair dryer, the letters melted back into the latex. Smith filmed the blister words disappearing, then ran the film backward so that the words seemed to be magically appearing on the stomach.

For scenes in which Blair's neck seemed to swell—and for the exploding head scene in *Scanners*—Smith devised an effects makeup technique that has since been used in many other films. An inflatable bladder, like a thick balloon, was attached to the body part that was supposed to swell or explode. The bladder was hidden by a layer of latex makeup, and air was pumped into it through hidden tubes. In the case of *Scanners*, the bladder attached to the character's forehead swelled to the bursting point, sending out a shower of fake blood.

Recent trends in effects makeup

For modern horror films, effects artists have learned that they can create double layers of a character's face or body with latex. One layer might look like normal skin, while a second layer can be made to look like the bloody flesh underneath the skin. In the Steven Spielberg production *Poltergeist*, for instance, a character appears to pull off chunks of his face. In fact, the face was a fake head with latex "skin" covering bloody-looking goo underneath. As the camera recorded a close shot of this head, Spielberg himself reached up from below camera range and ripped off chunks of the "face." It was

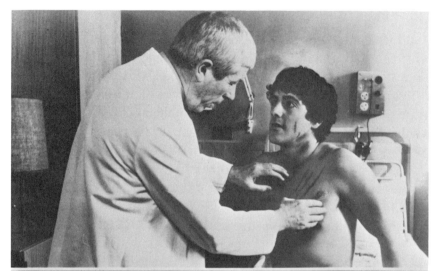

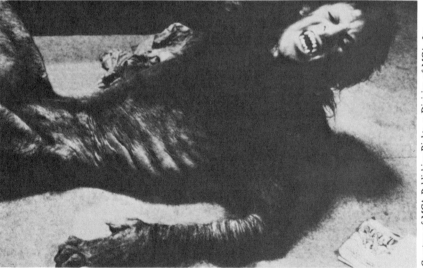

A dummy wolf body, latex masks, colored contact lenses, and inflatable bladders all contributed to Actor David Naughton's on-screen transformation into a werewolf. In 1982, makeup artist Rick Baker won the first academy award for special effects for his work in An American Werewolf in London.

Spielberg's hand that audiences saw in this scene, not the actor's.

Dick Smith's assistant on *The Exorcist* was a young makeup artist named Rick Baker. In 1982, Baker won the first Academy Award for effects makeup for his work on *An American Werewolf in London.* Baker used latex masks, colored contact lenses, inflatable bladders (to make latex hands and faces seem to grow), and a full-sized wolf-body dummy to transform actor David Naughton into a werewolf. As the transformation took place on-screen, Naughton's head seemed to be connected to the wolf-body dummy. In fact, the actor's own body was concealed beneath the dummy in a hole in the floor.

At the same time Baker was working on *American Werewolf*, a young friend of his was creating effects makeup for another werewolf film, *The Howling* (1981). Rob Bottin began his career as a special effects makeup artist when he was just fourteen years old. Bottin's teachers made a deal with him: if he would come to class in the morning, they would let him work with Rick Baker in the afternoon.

Actor Dan O'Herlihy as a lizard-like alien in The Last Starfighter. *Thanks to sophisticated special-effects makeup, the strange-looking starfighter looked human enough to be received warmly by movie audiences.*

"Rick was kind of a big brother and father to me," Bottin said. "He told me to lose weight, get a haircut, and be respectable. He raised me." Bottin made molds, trimmed rubber, and attached hair to the huge costume used in the 1976 remake of *King Kong*. He helped Baker create the characters for the cantina scene in *Star Wars*. This brief barroom scene proved to be very popular with audiences. At the time, however, neither Bottin nor Baker had seen a completed script. "Rick told me the story was about a bunch of monsters who get drunk in a bar," Bottin said. Bottin was worried that the film would be a flop, but the success of *Star Wars* gave his career a boost.

Rob Bottin and *The Thing*

Bottin went on to work on many low-budget films before he was hired by director John Carpenter to do effects makeup for *The Fog* (1980). Carpenter's 1982 film, *The Thing*, gave Bottin a chance to create some of the most startling effects makeup gags in the history of movies.

In one incredible series of shots, a character named Norris appears to suffer a heart attack and is placed on an operating table. As a doctor works to revive him, Norris's chest suddenly opens to reveal huge teeth. The teeth proceed to bite off the doctor's arms. Norris's head then falls off its body and drags itself along the floor with a ten-foot-long-tongue. Meanwhile, another head emerges from Norris's chest. The head on the floor eventually sprouts legs like a gigantic spider and is torched by a character wielding a flamethrower.

The scene was done with latex models, air bladders, and lots of fake blood and goo—including melted bubble gum inside the neck of a dummy of the actor playing the character Norris. Effects operators hidden under the operating table worked the giant teeth. They also pumped the blood through a fire extinguisher and stretched the dummy's neck until the head fell off the torso. The head seemed to pull itself across the floor by wrapping its tongue around a chair leg. Actually, it was being pulled in the opposite direction by wires attached to the back of the head. This caused the tongue to stretch out. The film was later run backward so that the tongue appeared to be pulling the head by reeling itself in.

The head with spider's legs was a latex model mounted on a tiny radio-controlled car. The legs were attached to the car's wheels so that they appeared to move up and down as the wheels turned. Rob Bottin tried to minimize the blood in this scene. ''If you had blood squirting all over in some of these scenes,'' Bottin said, ''I think you'd make people chuck [vomit].''

When director John Carpenter first saw this scene on film, his reaction was, ''Gimme a break, you guys!'' Carpenter knew, however, that his forty-member effects crew had come up with something special. They had crossed the line that normally separated makeup effects from other physical effects. The characters in this film were not being made up simply to look unusual—they were coming apart, blowing up, and changing shape right on screen. Bottin and his crew had used makeup effects to create a world that was completely impossible and yet completely believable.

CHAPTER TEN

The Shape of Things to Come

A powerful new tool is changing the ways special effects are made. That new tool is the computer. Some filmmakers envision a day when entire movies will be made by computer—without actors, sets, or cameras. Computers are already playing an important role in the production of television commercials and music videos. Computerized special effects in movies may soon be giving shape to new worlds of fantasy and adventure.

Westworld: the beginning of computerized special effects

In 1973, the makers of a film called *Westworld* wanted to show their audience how the world looked through the eyes of a robot. They hired an experimental filmmaker named John Whitney Jr. to design the robot's "point of view" scenes. Whitney's father, John Whitney Sr., had been the first filmmaker to work with computers. (He also was the inventor of the "streaking" effect used by Douglas Trumbull for the "stargate corridor" sequence in *2001*.)

John Whitney Jr. decided to use a technique developed by the Jet Propulsion Laboratory (JPL) in Pasadena, California. JPL had put together a computer linkup that allowed the Mariner space probe to send pictures of the planet Mars back to Earth.

Mariner was designed to photograph Mars, then turn the photographed images into series of numbers. Each image photographed by Mariner ended up looking like a paint-by-numbers picture, with a couple of big differences. In a paint-by-numbers picture, each part of the picture is given a number, and that number stands for a color. When the artist sees the number "3" on a picture of the sky, for instance, he or she knows to paint that part of the picture blue.

The Mariner computer broke up pictures in a similar fashion. Instead of dividing pictures into big areas like sky and land, however, it divided the pictures into thousands of tiny points. Instead of using colors, the computer used only black and white. The computer gave a number ("1" or "0") to every point in an image according to whether the point was black ("1") or white ("0").

When the points were combined, they also showed areas of gray. To get an idea of how this happened, look at a newspaper photo up close. It is made up of thousands of tiny black and white dots. From a distance the dots also form many shades of gray. The Mariner photos were made up of similar patterns of dots. Mariner sent its dot numbers back to Earth by an electronic signal. Using these numbers, the JPL computer on Earth could make copies of the "pictures" of Mars sent to it by Mariner.

John Whitney Jr. followed JPL's method of using computers to break down pictures into many points of lightness and darkness. In the process, he realized that he not only could make copies of *Westworld*'s filmed images, but could also change those images.

Special effects in *Westworld*

Whitney used his computer to add colors to black-and-white images. He switched lights to darks and vice versa. He came up with ways to stretch, squeeze, and twist images and to give the images unusual patterns. All of these changes could be used to create special effects images for *Westworld*.

For the robot's point of view in *Westworld*, Whitney decided to use one special pattern that his computer produced. He used the computer to turn images into "checkerboards." Each checkerboard image contained 3,600 separate rectangles. They looked something like a picture made out of bathroom tiles. Every time the *Westworld* robot looked at someone, the film showed that person as an image made up of hundreds of these tiny rectangles.

Whitney found that it was easiest for his computer to "see" high-contrast images, that is, images where darks and lights really stood out from each other. So, for some scenes, the filmmakers photographed actor Richard Benjamin while he was wearing some very unusual makeup. He was dressed in an all-white cowboy outfit, with white makeup on his face and hands, and white coloring in his hair. "He looked as though he had fallen into a barrel of flour!" said the film's cinematographer.

Benjamin was filmed against a dark background, so that he really

Actor Yul Brynner plays a gunslinging robot in Westworld. *High-tech computer images allow audiences to "see" through Brynner's mechanical eyes.*

Courtesy of Turner Entertainment

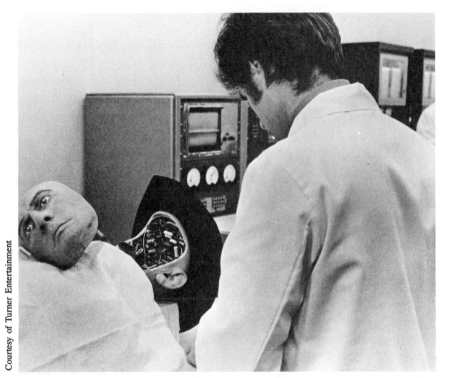

Courtesy of Turner Entertainment

A technician repairs the malfunctioning robot in Westworld. *The robot looks so much like actor Yul Brynner that audiences have difficulty telling them apart.*

stood out. This high-contrast image was then fed into Whitney's computer. Once the image was in the computer, Whitney could break it down into the pattern of tiny rectangles. Then he added different colors. The resulting image looked like Benjamin was being watched through a patterned glass screen—the screen of the robot's mechanical eyeball.

The computer images that John Whitney Jr. designed as special effects for *Westworld* were meant to look "computerized." Since the film's robot was supposed to be a sophisticated computer itself, it was natural for it to "see" things the way Whitney's computer did. The next step for Whitney was to use the computer to create images that looked more like real life.

Whitney went to work for a company called "Triple-I": Information International Incorporated. In 1982, Triple-I became one of three companies hired by Walt Disney Studios to produce computerized special effects for the movie *TRON*. *TRON* was the first full-length film to use a large amount of computer-generated imagery.

Flynn is trapped

TRON is the story of a computer programmer named Flynn who accidentally gets transported into the electronic world inside his computer. Once inside the computer, Flynn is forced to compete at deadly games—including a fast-paced race on streaking motorcycles called "light cycles"—in order to defeat the evil "Master Control Program."

Disney Studio's Bill Kroyer and Jerry Rees were *TRON*'s computer image "choreographers." Their job was to imagine the way scenes should look. They then gave instructions to the computer programmers at Triple-I and the other computer effects companies working on *TRON*. Kroyer and Rees "choreographed" scenes—they built them up from their imaginations—the way a ballet master choreographs a dance.

Kroyer and Rees asked the computer technicians to supply *TRON* with both backgrounds and solid objects, such as the racing light cycles. They found out that the computer could make the light cycles do "impossible" maneuvers, such as right-angle turns at high speeds. The computer could also create a sunless world in which every object could still be seen clearly. It could surround real human characters with machines and spaceships that existed only in the computer. It could even make the image look like it had been shot with a moving camera.

"You can move the camera anywhere you want," Kroyer said.

"There is no limitation; you can blow things up; you can move things at any speed; make 90-degree turns; you can have things completely disobey the laws of gravity or. . .anything. It's a great feeling of power." Although its images still did not look like "the real world," *TRON* did demonstrate a whole new range of computer-generated special effects.

After leaving Triple-I, Whitney formed a new company called Digital Productions. Digital Productions used the world's most powerful computer, the Cray Supercomputer, to perform the 75 million calculations needed to produce one frame (one twenty-fourth of a second) of "realistic-looking" film. For *The Last Starfighter* (1984), Digital Productions developed spaceships that were as realistic looking as the miniatures filmed by motion-control for the *Star Wars* films.

Using the latest high-tech computers, whole scenes can be created with computer-generated images that look as real as actual models. This space fleet in The Last Starfighter *is a computer-made image.*

Yet *The Last Starfighter*'s spaceships were images completely created by computer.

For *Westworld*, Whitney had used a computer in place of an optical printer, to change images that had already been filmed. For *The Last Starfighter*, he used a computer in place of matte paintings and miniatures, to create objects and backgrounds. In the future, he hopes to use a computer in place of a camera and actors. He hopes to create entirely new movies that exist only in the mind of the artist and the "mind" of the computer.

"Our notion," Whitney says, "is to use the computer to create lifelike characters who are modeled after known personalities. We may be able to re-create stars of the past—Clark Gable or Rita Hayworth—cast them in new roles, bring them forward in time into new settings."

Computer use at ILM

The goal at Industrial Light and Magic also is to use computers to create real-looking objects, and someday even people. The technicians at ILM, however, think it will be a long time before computers can produce entire motion pictures—as opposed to individual images—that look like the real world. In the meantime, ILM's computer division is concentrating on using computers to create special effects shots that can be added to films that have been photographed in the normal way.

Matte artist Chris Evans was the first person ILM called on to design computerized images. Evans "painted" his computerized images at an electronic paint station. This electronic paint station was a clear white board that was sensitive to light. When a strong light was shined on the board, the board responded by sending an electronic message into a computer.

Instead of a paintbrush, Evans used a "light pen," a pen that gave off a strong, thin beam of light. The lines Evans drew with the light pen were picked up by the paint station board, fed into a computer, and displayed on a television screen. It took a while for Evans to train himself to look at the screen (where his image was appearing) rather than the board (which remained blank) while he "painted."

Evans worked with computer programmer Tom Porter to refine the computer program that allowed him to "paint" images. Together, they made working with a light pen more like working with a paintbrush. After a while, the computer knew when Evans wanted a line to be thick and heavy, like a firm brush stroke, or fine and thin, like a soft, delicate stroke with a paintbrush.

The result of Evans's work was a sixty-second series of images used in *Star Trek II: The Wrath of Khan*. In the film, Captain Kirk watches a videotape in order to learn about Project Genesis, the scientific invention that is supposed to create life on barren planets. The tape shows a dark planet that catches fire, cools off, then develops rivers, oceans, plants, and other life forms.

Audiences watching *Star Trek II* were not supposed to notice that a brand-new computerized special effect—Evans's computer painting—had been used in making the Project Genesis tape. Viewers were supposed to think that this tape was the kind of thing Captain Kirk watched all the time. Evans therefore designed his work to blend with the rest of the film. It took Evans and nine other ILM computer operators five months to produce the Project Genesis tape.

A knight comes to life

For *Young Sherlock Holmes* (1985), ILM's special effects artists designed a more complicated image than the Project Genesis tape. Under Dennis Muren's supervision, the ILM computer artists created a stained-glass knight in armor. In the movie, the knight comes to life, leaps out of his stained-glass window, and chases a priest out of a church. Throughout the sequence, the knight actually appears to be made of thin panes of glass.

The stained-glass knight was first "drawn" on the computer's electronic paint station. Then the image was transferred directly to film through the use of a powerful laser beam. This represented an important new step in computer effects technology. Prior to *Young Sherlock Holmes*, computer images were filmed by displaying the images on a very bright television screen, then photographing the screen with a movie camera. Using a laser beam to print the computer image directly onto film was a more difficult process, but it resulted in clearer images and brighter colors.

ILM's special effects designers still prefer to use miniatures rather than computer-generated images for most scenes that involve moving objects like spaceships. ILM is trying, however, to use computerized special effects in place of brief, hand-drawn animation effects. These are effects that are actually painted into scenes by ILM artists.

Electrical effects are difficult

Many "electrical" effects in movies—from Luke Skywalker's "light saber" (his glowing sword) to the lightning bolts that consume Queen Bavmorda in *Willow*—are actually drawn by hand and added to films long after the scenes are shot. The process is very time-consuming, since the artist must draw the effect separately for every frame of film. That means that twenty-four different drawings are needed for every second that the shot is on-screen.

Computer animation—using the computer to draw images—can save time and create even more spectacular special effects. The spinning, changing, three-dimensional map that seems to leap out at the rebel troops when they gather in the briefing room in *Return of the Jedi* is a product of computer animation.

The transformation of the good sorceress Fin Raziel in *Willow* was also done partly through computer animation. Changing Raziel's face from a woman's to that of a tiger was accomplished by ILM's computer artists. For *Who Framed Roger Rabbit* (1988), ILM's special effects artists used computers to make hand-drawn cartoon characters look three-dimensional—not flat, but really standing out from the streets and buildings in the background.

Like all cartoon characters, Roger Rabbit was first drawn by hand on a flat, clear sheet of plastic. Every time Roger changed position, a new drawing had to be made. Twelve separate images of Roger were drawn for every second he was on-screen. These images where then filmed with a movie camera. When projected onto a screen, the images flowed together (at the rate of twenty-four frames per second), and the character seemed to be moving. These cartoon images were later layered together with shots of real people, like detective Eddie Valiant, and real objects, many of which were shot against blue screens.

The ILM computer was used to give Roger a fuller, rounder shape. The process used by ILM's computer artists was similar to John Whitney Jr.'s stretching and twisting of images in his experiments for *Westworld*. The computer also enabled ILM's animators to add shadows to the surface of Roger's figure, as if the sun's rays were bouncing off his body and clothes. This made Roger look as solid and three-dimensional as the humans around him.

The "invisible" art

Throughout the history of motion pictures, the goal of special effects artists has been to make "impossible" scenes look real. Special effects can save filmmakers time and money. They make it possible for movies to transport audiences into exciting, frightening, dreamlike new worlds. Special effects allow audiences to live out their fears and fantasies.

Some effects are created with simple, everyday materials, such as pea soup and cleaning fluid. Others need the more complex artistry of computers. But all require the creative genius of the human mind.

As a new generation of filmmakers begins to work with computers, the nature of special effects may change. The special effects discussed in this book have been used most often in movies of fantasy and adventure like *King Kong* and *Star Wars*. Computers will allow special effects to be added to more realistic-looking films. Films that deal with real people in real situations may someday be made more inexpensively and more dramatically through the use of computers.

Computers may also make it possible for a growing number of young film artists to express their unique, personal views of the world. Steven Spielberg made his first feature-length film when he was sixteen years old. He used a tiny eight-millimeter movie camera. If Spielberg were a teenager today, he would probably be filming with a video camera and creating special effects with a home computer and an electronic paint station.

Special effects artists may like their work to look invisible on-screen—but that does not mean that the techniques of special effects should be kept secret. If more people know about special effects, then more people will be able to use them in their own films and videotapes. More people will appreciate the lengths to which filmmakers go just to entertain their audiences. And the next time Indiana Jones is caught in some impossibly dangerous trap, more viewers will be able to turn to their friends and say, "I know how they did that."

Glossary

blue screen method: filming people or objects against the background of a large screen lit with blue light; through a series of steps involving an optical printer, the blue background can be removed, leaving "cut out" figures of the characters or objects, which can then be "pasted into" other scenes.

computer animation: using a computer to "draw" images; this may be done either by giving the computer patterns of numbers which describe different points in the image, or by drawing with a beam of light on a light-sensitive surface (or "paint station") connected to the computer.

double expose: filming two separate images on the same section of film to make it look like the images were in the same location at the same time. For example, filming a car in a parking lot and then filming a mountain scene on the same section of film to make it look like the car is in the mountains.

Dykstraflex: one of the earliest **motion-control camera systems**, developed by John Dykstra to film special effects for *Star Wars*.

effects makeup: elaborate makeup that drastically changes an actor's appearance.

frame: one of a series of images on a strip of film.

frozen: a way of describing a moving picture image that has been turned into a still photograph, usually through the use of an **optical printer**.

glass shot: a "live" image blended with a painting (for instance, characters walking through a painted landscape); the live action is shot through a clear plate of glass which has been partly covered with a painting.

"go-motion" animation: filming models or miniatures (as in **stop-motion** animation) while the models are actually being moved by rods attached to a computer-guided machine; this process more realistically captures the slightly blurred movement that the camera normally records when filming live characters.

latex: liquid rubber used to make masks or models; it also can be applied to actors in thin layers to change their appearances.

live-action shot: a sequence of film using real people and scenery rather than artificial effects and animation.

matte: any object held in front of a camera to block out part of the scene being filmed. The blocked-out part can be filled in later with scenery, characters, or action shots that have been filmed separately.

matte line: a glowing line around a figure which has been combined, through the use of mattes, with a separately photographed background.

matte painting: painting of a scene on canvas, fiberboard, or glass used to block out and replace part of another scene being filmed.

miniature: a greatly reduced model of a vehicle, character, animal, object, or location that can be photographed and made to appear life-size or larger.

model: a dummy or replica substituted for a live actor or real object.

motion-control camera system: a motion picture camera whose movements and shifts in focus are electronically controlled by a computer, so that they may be repeated exactly over and over again; motion-control systems permit filmmakers to film different parts of a scene separately (for instance, individual spaceships, asteroids, and laser blasts as part of a space battle) and still have each part of the scene appear in just the right place on the screen when the different shots are combined.

optical effects: trick photography that makes things appear different than they really are.

optical printer: a machine in which a moving picture projector is placed opposite a camera, so that a projected image may be photographed a second time; by this means, an image may be **frozen**, made larger or smaller, combined with other images, turned upside down, or changed in other ways.

physical effects: effects that actually take place in front of the camera. Common examples are fires and explosions.

rear projection: projecting a background scene onto a screen behind actors so it appears that the actors are in that location.

silhouette: solid black figure in the shape of an actor. Used as a **traveling matte** to block out the actor's image.

split-screen matte: a **matte** used to block out and replace portions of the screen so that images filmed at different times and places can be combined and shown together. For example, a split-screen matte allows two actors in different locations to be shown together on-screen, talking to each other on the telephone.

squib: tiny explosive charge used to look like a bullet explosion.

stop-motion animation: **models** and **miniatures** made to look as if they are moving by making small adjustments in their positions and filming each adjustment. For example, small adjustments might be made in the legs of a model gorilla and each adjustment filmed to make it look as if the gorilla were walking.

storyboard: series of drawings made by artists to show how each scene will look on film.

"streaking": a visual effect in which moving objects are filmed so that tails of light trail behind them.

stuntmen or **stuntwomen:** special actors who substitute for the actors during dangerous scenes involving stunts.

three-D: a type of motion picture photography that gives an added feeling of depth (or "three-dimensionality") to the image, often making people or objects appear to "pop out of" the screen.

traveling matte: an optical process that blacks out the part of a filmed image where a moving character or object will later be added.

Bibliography

American Cinematographer, ''Behind the Scenes of Westworld,'' November 1973, pp. 1394 ff.

Kay Anderson, *''Star Trek: The Wrath of Khan*: How the TV Series Became a Hit Movie, At Last,'' *Cinefantastique*, v.12, n.5-6, July/August 1982, pp. 51-75.

Michael Cieply and Charles Solomon, ''Fantasy Wizards Pull 'Rabbit' Out of Their Hat,'' San Francisco Chronicle *Datebook* June 19, 1988, p. 19.

Frederick S. Clarke, ''The 3-D Explosion,'' *Cinefantastique*, v.13, n.6/ v.14, n.1, September 1983, pp. 28-32.

Bruce Cook, ''Close Encounters with Steven Spielberg,'' *American Film*, November 1977, pp.24-29.

Robert P. Everett, ''Hell and High Water,'' *Cinefex*, n.18, August 1984, pp.4-41.

Raymond Fielding, *The Technique of Special Effects Cinematography.* London/Boston: Focal Press, 1985.

Christopher Finch, *Special Effects: Creating Movie Magic.* NY: Abbeville Press, 1984.

Ron Fry and Pamela Fourzon, *The Saga of Special Effects.* Englewood Cliffs, NJ: Prentice-Hall, Inc., 1977.

Paul R. Gagne, "*Creepshow*: Masters of the Macabre," *Cinefantastique,* September/October, 1982, pp.17-35.

Paul R. Gagne, "Dick Smith on *The Hunger*," *Cinefantastique*, v.13, n.4, April/May 1983, pp.16-23.

Louis Giannetti, *Understanding Movies.* Englewood Cliffs, NJ: Prentice-Hall, 1972.

Ron Haver, "Merian C. Cooper: First King of Kong," *American Film,* December/January 1977, pp.14-23.

David J. Hogan, "I don't know what it is, but it's weird and pissed off," *Cinefantastique*, v.13, n.2-3, November/December 1982, pp.48-75.

David J. Hogan, "*Jaws 3-D*," *Cinefantastique,* v.13, n.6/ v.14, n.1, September 1983, pp.56-73.

David Hutchison, "*TRON: Changing the Laws of Physics*," *Starlog*, n.62, September 1982, pp.50-55.

Alan McKenzie and Derek Ware, *Hollywood Tricks of the Trade.* NY: Gallery Books, 1986.

Brad Munson, "The Last Voyage of the Starship Enterprise," *Cinefex*, n.18, August 1984, pp.42-67.

Dale Pollock, *Skywalking: The Life and Films of George Lucas.* NY: Harmony Books, 1983.

Stephen Rebello, "*Something Wicked This Way Comes*," *Cinefantastique*, v.13, n.5, June/July 1983, pp.28-49.

Paul M. Sammon, "The Making of *Blade Runner*," *Cinefantastique*, v.12, n.5-6, July/August 1982, pp.20-47.

Jody Duncan Shannon, "Cheap and Cheesy and Off-the-Cuff: The Effects of Beetlejuice," *Cinefex*, n.34, May 1988, pp.4-43.

Thomas G. Smith, *Industrial Light and Magic: The Art of Special Effects.* NY: Ballantine Books, 1986.

George Turner, "Howard Hawks' *The Thing*," *Cinefantastique*, v.12, n.5-6, July/August 1982, pp.79-85.

John Whitney Jr., "Creating the Special Effects for *Westworld*," *American Cinematographer*, November 1973, pp.1477-80.

Index

Picture Credits

Cover: Photofest
Courtesy of Turner Entertainment
© 1984 MGM/UA Entertainment Co.
Academy of Motion Picture Arts and Sciences, 63
"Planet of the Apes" © 1967, Apjac Productions, Inc. and Twentieth
Century-Fox Film Corporation. All Rights Reserved, 81
© 1945 Beverly Productions, Inc. All Rights Reserved, Courtesy of The
Samuel Goldwyn Company, 30
Courtesy of Boss Film Corporation, 36, 40, 49, 50
© 1963 Columbia Pictures Industries, Inc. All Rights Reserved, 52
"King Kong" © 1976, by Dino De Laurentiis Corporation. All Rights
Reserved, 46, 59
Ealing Studios, Ltd., 14, 15, 51, 75
Courtesy of J-K Camera Engineering Co., 65
TM © Lucasfilm Ltd. (LFL) 1980. All Rights Reserved, 56
TM © Lucasfilm Ltd. (LFL) 1983. All Rights Reserved, 33, 34, 42
TM © Lucasfilm Ltd. (LFL) 1984. All Rights Reserved, 21
© 1968 Metro-Goldwyn-Mayer, Inc., 29, 64
© 1973 Metro-Goldwyn-Mayer, Inc., 90, 91
Museum of Modern Art/Film Stills Archives, 20, 90
Jerry Ohlinger's Movie Materials Store, Inc., 30, 85, 93
Photofest, 12, 23, 29, 52, 64, 81, 91
© 1933 RKO Radio Pictures, Inc. Ren. 1960 RKO Radio Pictures, Inc., a
Division of RKO General, Inc., 47
© 1939 Selznick International Pictures, Inc. Ren. 1967 Metro-Goldwyn-
Mayer, Inc., 74
Springer/Bettmann Film Archives, 72
"The Towering Inferno" © 1974, Twentieth Century-Fox Film Corporation
and Warner Bros. Inc. All Rights Reserved, 72
Copyright © by Universal Pictures, a Division of Universal City Studios,
Inc. Courtesy of MCA Publishing Rights, a Division of MCA Inc., 23, 58,
79, 80, 84, 85, 93
UPI/Bettmann Newsphotos, 68
Wisconsin Center for Film and Theater Research, 14, 15, 47, 51, 58, 75, 79

About the Author

The wicked queen in Disney's *Snow White* gave Tom Powers his first movie scare when he was five years old. He has been ducking under seats at movies ever since.

Mr. Powers holds a B.A. in English literature from Yale University and a Master of Arts in Film Studies from San Francisco State University. He has published fifteen books for children and young adults, including *Champions of Change: Biographies of Famous Hispanic Americans*, *Reading Geography*, and recent books on *Monster Movies* and *Horror Movies*.

He currently teaches motion picture history at Ohio State University. His courses include a popular class on the social and psychological significance of special effects in movies.